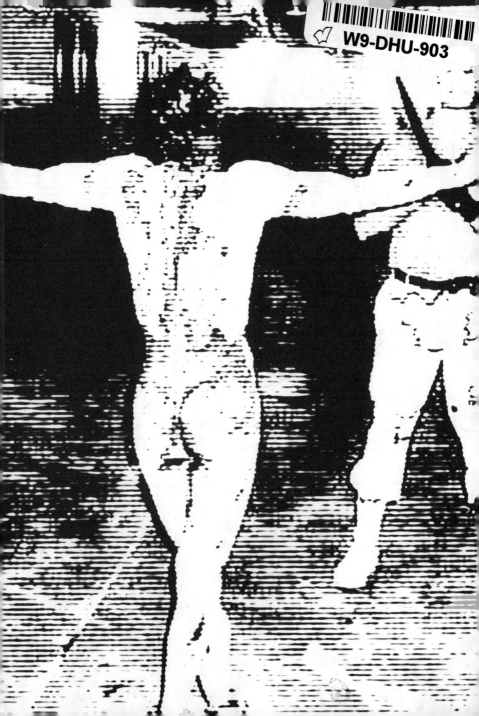

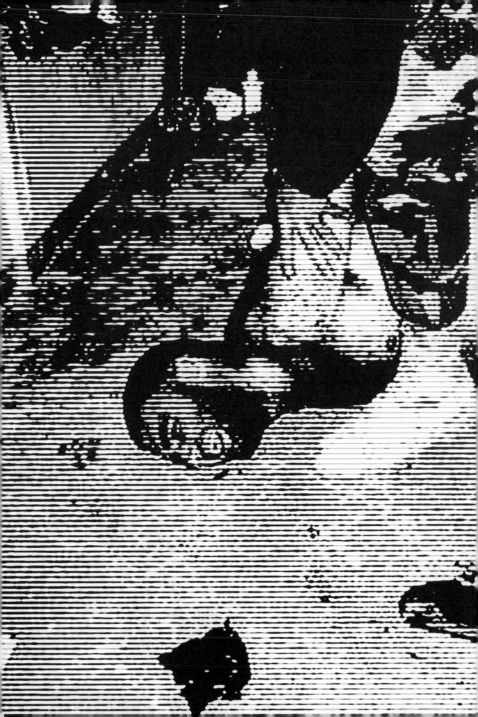

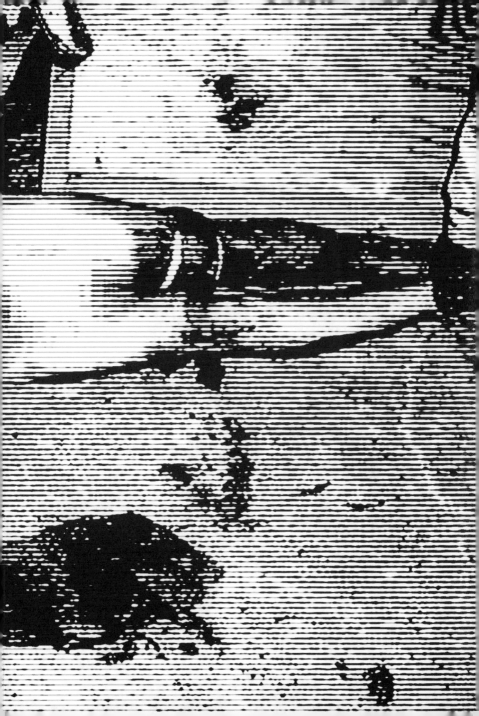

A Good War is Hard to Find

The Art of Violence in America

. . . .

David Griffith

SOFT SKULL PRESS

BROOKLYN NY 2006

CONTENTS

Mrs. Shortley recalled a newsreel she had once seen of a small room piled high with bodies of dead naked people all in a heap, their arms and legs tangled together, a head thrust in here, a head there, a foot, a knee, a part that should have been covered up sticking out, a hand raised clutching nothing. Before you could realize that it was real and take it into your head, the picture changed and a hollow-sounding voice was saying, "Time marches on!"

. . . .

Flannery O'Connor, "The Displaced Person"

Baghdad
January 17, 1991

I

. . . .

Symphony No. 1
(In Memoriam, Dresden, 1945)

THE DAY THE BOMBS STARTED FALLING ON BAGHDAD my Notre Dame jacket, a dark-blue satin jacket with NOTRE DAME stitched across the front and a pugilistic leprechaun on the sleeve—my most prized possession—was stolen out of my locker. They also stole a package of Hostess SnoBalls and a peanut butter and honey sandwich, snacks that I would eat after school to give me energy for wrestling practice. I weighed 110 pounds and wrestled in the 112-pound weight class.

A young policewoman came to the house to take a report. It was maybe seven in the evening. Before the policewoman arrived I was sitting downstairs in the dim living room trying to do my algebra homework but, instead, watching live images of explosions lighting up the Baghdad skyline.

It was impossible to understand what was happening on the screen. There were no soldiers. My picture of war came from Vietnam: shaky handheld-camera footage of soldiers cautiously trudging through the jungle.

Instead, what I saw was a view of Central Baghdad from a hotel rooftop, narrated by journalists who had chosen to stay in the city even after being warned of the danger. The journalists, Peter Arnett and Bernard Shaw, tried to communicate what it felt like to see these images, rating the power of each bomb blast based on how violently the windows rattled or the hotel swayed. At times the burst of light as a bomb detonated made the screen go completely white. I couldn't keep my eyes off the television.

When the policewoman came downstairs she started watching the footage too. She looked stunned, as though she'd never seen a television. "They're bombing Baghdad," I said. "Wow," she said.

The entire time the woman took my statement about the stolen jacket her eyes cut back and forth between the note pad in her hand and the television.

I got the jacket back. One day I was walking down the hall at school and a kid passed me wearing the jacket. "That's my jacket," I said. "No, it's not," the kid sneered. One of the deans of the school happened to walk by at this moment and asked what the problem was. "Look in the sleeves," I told him. My mother had written GRIFFITH in permanent black marker in each sleeve. Sure enough, when the dean turned the right sleeve inside out, there was my name.

Things were like that then. Open and shut. Yes it is. No it isn't. Everything seemed good, clean and orderly. I learned that there was such a thing as justice—I had witnessed it.

At night, I was learning that war could be humane and just. Night after night, first-person footage from the nose of smart bombs allowed me to see with my own eyes that American bombers weren't dumping their payloads indiscriminately over cities, like the Germans did to Britain and the Brits did to Germany and we did to the Japanese during World War II. These were "smart" bombs. This was a "smart" war in all the various connotations of "smart": intelligent; shrewd and calculating; amusingly clever; with a neat and well-cared-for appearance; fashionable and stylish; vigorous and brisk; causing a sharp stinging sensation.

Our history teacher didn't talk about the Gulf War. She didn't even pull down a map of the world and point to the Middle East so that we at least knew where it was taking place. Then again, I suppose she had bigger problems to worry about—some kids in the class couldn't locate Illinois on a map.

Neither do I remember talking about the war with my friends, unless it was to ask whether we'd seen the latest awesome press conference footage—General Schwarzkopf standing in front of a television monitor narrating the flight of a bomb as it entered the chimney of a building or through the window of a munitions depot.

Oddly enough, I thought about the war the most when I was at band practice. That fall, the band director, a man named Scott Casagrande, passed out the sheet music for *Symphony No. 1 (In Memoriam, Dresden, 1945)* a piece by Daniel Bukvich dedicated to the firebombing and subsequent obliteration of the German city of Dresden. One look at the part in front of me and I could tell that this was unlike anything I'd played before. The parts were written aleatorically, meaning that, instead of notes on the staff creating a melody and countermelody, there were diagrams and instructions telling us to play our instruments in unorthodox ways to represent the bombing of the city. The trombones were to drone on a low B flat to mimic the rumble of bombers approaching the city. The trumpets sounded the wailing air-raid sirens. Next the score instructed the entire band to frantically whisper the word "firestorm" over and over in German, to capture the panicked gossip that spread through the city as the first wave of bombers dropped jellied gasoline in order to prepare the way for the incendiary bombs that would ignite the city.

The trombone drone of the bombers continued as the flutes began mimicking the sound of bombs whistling toward the earth. The percussion section commanded a whole battery of drums to conjure up the bomb blasts and shook thunder out of a sheet of metal. As Dresden burned, we blew air through our horns to create the violent winds, brought on by the rapidly rising heat, that sucked victims into the burning rubble of buildings and blew over structures weakened by the initial blasts. When it was all done, roughly thirty thousand civilians had been killed, many buried alive in basement bomb shelters and then burned beyond recognition by the great fire that raged for weeks to come. After playing the piece, I always felt emotionally drained and distant, as though I had experienced something traumatic, felt the presence of a darker reality.

I don't remember when I first had the idea, but at some point I approached Mr. Casagrande and asked him if I could find some images that could be projected on a screen above the band while we played. I have to believe that this idea wouldn't have come to me without the live war footage I took in every night on CNN. I was not a technologically savvy kid. (I used to hold a tape recorder up to the television to record my favorite songs from MTV.) But hearing this music, I saw images.

At the public library I found photos from books on World War II: bombers in flight, photos of bombs falling in a cluster, aerial photos of the majestic city of Dresden with its Baroque domes and soaring spires. I found photos of the city on fire, photos of the smoldering, wrecked buildings and, finally, photos of a wooden cart piled with scorched black corpses.

The AV director, Mr. Baldwin, made the photos into slides, and then, over the course of several rehearsals, I sequenced them to the music, so that the image of bombers corresponded to the droning of the trombones, the falling bombs corresponded to the whistling of the flutes, and so on.

On the night of the performance, I stood back behind the heavy, black curtain at the rear of the stage with my finger on the button of the slide projector. I began with a picture of the city before the bombing and then toggled back and forth between the image of the bombers in flight and the cluster of bombs falling toward earth in order to give the sensation of many bombers dropping many bombs.

I felt powerful, like the Great Oz, proud to be inspiring fear in this audience of parents and school administrators, perhaps disturbing their pat notions of war and its costs. In some ways I've been trying to get back to that feeling ever since—trying to find moments where what I'm hearing and what I'm seeing come together to reveal a disturbing truth.

However, I must confess, at no point as I stood behind that curtain was I consciously thinking of the war in Iraq. Dresden was different, I told myself. Dresden was butchery, barbarity. The bombing of Iraq, as I saw on television every night for a few months, was clean, efficient, just.

Patient Name: _____ File # _____ Date: _____

PAIN CHART

Using the appropriate symbols,
mark the areas of the body where you feel the described sensations.
Include ALL affected areas.

Numbness	+++++
Burning	XXXXX
Pins and Needles	OOOOO
Sharp	/////
Dull and Aching	✱✱✱✱✱
Stabbing	☆☆☆
Weakness	△△△△△

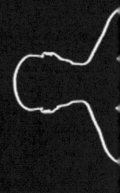

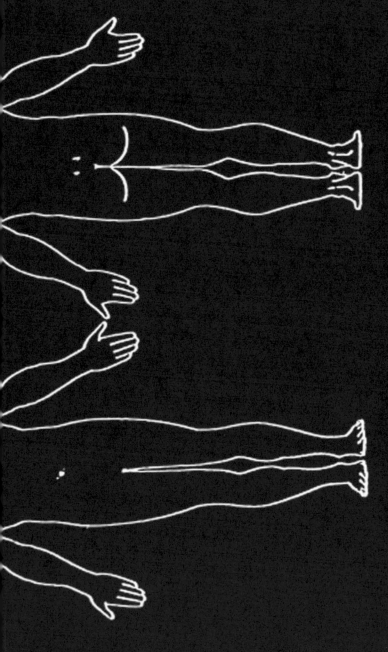

Patient Signature:

~ Over Please ~

A Good War is Hard to Find: Flannery O'Connor, Abu Ghraib, and the Problem of American Innocence

IT IS FOUR DAYS BEFORE CHRISTMAS, 2004. Earlier today, a U.S. base in the northern Iraqi city of Mosul was bombed. At least two dozen are dead, the latest casualties of an insurgency that seems to be gaining zeal as the first fully-democratic Iraqi elections in over thirty years approach. It is an insurgency born, in part, by what the Bush administration has been calling the "catastrophic success" of the land war that ended—mission accomplished—now over nineteen months ago. It is an insurgency—a phantom, freedom-hating force—made up of innumerable guerrilla outfits without uniforms, flags or discernable national identity.

What unifies them, according to many, are the abusive practices of the occupying force. Nowhere are these allegations more visible and, perhaps, well-founded than the photos that have emerged from Abu Ghraib prison.

The photos from Abu Ghraib have catalyzed a new generation of politically-motivated Iraqi artists. A large-scale mural on a wall in Baghdad's Sadr City reproduces the image of the naked and hooded detainee, standing atop a box, electrical wires attached to his fingers. Next to him stands the Statue of Liberty, dressed in a white robe and hood reminiscent of the Klan's famous disguises, poised to throw the switch that will send electricity singing through the wires. A more formal gathering of this new art could be seen at the Hewar Art Gallery in the Wazerieh district of central Baghdad. In June of 2004, twenty-five artists showed their work; the image of the hooded detainee is reflected over and over in plaster and marble sculptures, paintings and installation pieces. The image speaks to the perceived corruption of the American occupation and the deep hypocrisy of America, a nation founded on religious tolerance, compassion and universal justice.

President Bush, in response to suggestions that the United States has lost the respect of the world community because of Abu Ghraib and the detainment of "unlawful combatants" at Guantanamo Bay, Cuba, said at a press conference on December 20th that the United States is a "nation of laws," and that the recent Supreme Court decision to grant Guantanamo detainees their right to the writ of habeas corpus proves the nation's dedication to justice. Any allegations of abuse are being investigated and taken seriously.

But are the Abu Ghraib photos and the allegations of abuse at Guantanamo just a matter of a few American troops, a few "bad apples," acting on their own, or is the picture-taking more widespread: are digital pictures part of new interrogation protocols tailored to exploit Muslim cultural values?

CIA, Department of Defense and Justice Department memos squabbling over the definition of torture, condoning low-grade torture in the war against terrorism, confirm that there is no clear policy stating how prisoners in the War on Terror should be treated.

The Abu Ghraib photos, as well as countless other allegations of abuse and torture, are evidence of the shadowy boundary between legal and immoral.

So what do the Abu Ghraib photos actually show us? Cropped, yes, the pictures suggest the work of only a handful of reservists. But uncropped they show more soldiers, some identified as military intelligence officers, standing around, a few watching, others preoccupied with the most mundane activities. One picture reveals a man cleaning his fingernails.

Images of such crass disregard become more than just evidence. They become icons, Rorschachs used by commentators to justify, criticize or deconstruct the war and the United States.

Many of the pictures resemble grotesque political cartoons: human pyramids, a prisoner in a cruciform pose atop a box with red wires curling away from his fingers, prisoners pantomiming sexual acts, prisoners cowering before attack dogs. They're impossible caricatures, their effects exaggerated when removed from the larger, more complicated context of the war. They are images even the most zealous anti-war cartoonist would feel uneasy imagining, let alone sketching. And there are hundreds of unreleased photos that have been blocked by the Pentagon due to their outrageousness, their ability to inspire perhaps an all out Holy War. Scenes of rape and even murder.

Some commentators—mostly conservatives, such as Robert Knight of Concerned Women for America, but even left-wing social critic Susan Sontag—cited our society's addiction to hard-core pornography to explain the scandal. Why else would the abuse have included so much nudity, sex, and sadomasochism—and exhibitionism, in the form of extensive photo and video documentation? In their view, the prison was an outpost of our debased, porn-soaked culture.

Consider the two main protagonists in this spectacle: Army Corporal Charles Graner, Jr., an alleged wife beater, once divorced, now serving ten years in a military prison for his role as the so-called ringleader of the late-night abuse, and Army Pfc. Lynndie England, seen giving exuberant thumbs-up gestures while standing in front of naked, hooded prisoners, now serving three years for mistreating prisoners. (Some of the unreleased photos are said to show England having sex with other MPs.)

Military defense lawyers attempted to paint Graner, England and the rest as duty-bound reservists who were following orders from their superiors, whose apparent zeal portrayed in the photos was the result of extreme psychological duress: the pressures of guarding so many prisoners, the nightly mortar attacks, the knowledge that fellow soldiers were dying due to the lack of intelligence. After all, psychological experiments have proved that anyone, given the right conditions, can become a torturer, right? In this scenario, the abuse is reduced to a problem of abnormal psychology.

But moral and psychological interpretations of the scandal— usually in the service of ideology—fall short. There's another tragic, spiritual sense in which to understand the disturbing images of Abu Ghraib, a view formed by notions of innocence, sin and grace.

. .

CATHOLIC WRITER FLANNERY O'CONNOR would have considered the images of the prison scandal grotesque, but not in what she called "the pejorative sense," of just plain ugliness and ignorance. For O'Connor—whose characters are some of the most memorable grotesqueries in American literature—the grotesque makes visible hidden "discrepancies" between character and belief. Such images "connect or combine or embody two points; one is a point in the concrete and the other is a point not visible to the naked eye."

Take Cpl. Graner, for example. His pick-up truck still parked in the driveway of his Uniontown, Pennsylvania home at the time the pictures broke into the news, bears a license plate with the word Jesus and a picture of a cross. There is also a smooth stone in, appropriately enough, a "weed-choked" flower bed in front of his house, painted with a verse from the book of Hosea: "Sow for yourselves righteousness, reap the fruit of unfailing love and break up your unplowed ground; for it is time to see the Lord, until he comes and showers righteousness on you." [Hosea 10:12 NIV]

This stone is mentioned in most of the early news coverage of the scandal, treated as a bit of profound irony, the kind of coincidence newspaper reporters salivate over. How could a man with this bit of scripture displayed in his "postage-stamp" of a front yard, as one Pittsburgh weekly described it, commit such atrocious acts? It's an irony the media isn't equipped to engage at any depth.

Such ironies are the stuff of O'Connor's stories. Her characters think of themselves as Christians or otherwise good people, but their actions or attitudes reveal otherwise. Their pride blinds them to their own flaws, and only violence—usually from an unlikely source—opens their eyes, and offers them a chance at redemption.

For O'Connor, her native American South was the perfect landscape against which to paint her grotesque figures. But to Catholics in the 1950s, O'Connor's fascination with bizarre characters from the nation's most Protestant region was unsettling. She addressed their "certain impatience" with her work in 1963 at a speaking engagement at Georgetown University, in a speech titled "The Catholic Novelist in the Protestant South":

> The American Catholic trusts the fictional imagination about as little as he trusts anything. Before it's well on its feet, he's busy looking for heresy in it. The Catholic press is constantly broken out in a rash of articles on the failure of the Catholic novelist. The Catholic novelist is failing to reflect the virtue of hope, failing to show the Church's interest in social justice, failing to show life as a positive good, failing to portray our beliefs in a light that will make them desirable to others.

O'Connor accounts for this by accusing the Catholic reader of "being more Manichean than the Church permits...by separating nature from grace."

"Manichaeism"—or Dualism—was a third-century religion inspired by a Persian, Mani. It claimed the universe was governed by two, eternal, separate—and equal—forces: Good and Evil. Dualism has a certain attraction for Christians. In fact, in his *Mere Christianity*, C.S. Lewis said, "I personally think that next to Christianity, Dualism is the manliest and most sensible creed on the market." But, Lewis continued, "It has a catch to it." Lewis, drawing from St. Augustine and St. Thomas Aquinas, does his usual brilliant job of refuting Dualism—that the one eternal principle in Christianity, God, is good, that everything God made is good, and that evil is merely a perversion of the good:

> And do you now begin to see why Christianity has always said that the devil is a fallen angel? That is not a mere story for children. It is a real recognition of the fact that evil is a parasite, not an original thing. The powers that enable evil to carry on are powers given to it by goodness. All the things which enable man to be effectively bad are in themselves good things—resolution, cleverness, good looks, existence itself. That is why dualism, in a strict sense, will not work.

How to account for evil, then? Lewis continues: "God created things which have free will. That means creatures which can go either wrong or right." Evil is the pursuit of good things—pleasure, love, money, power, "by the wrong method."

That's O'Connor territory. Her stories reveal the hidden evil residing in the human heart, the pursuit of good that masks a secret pride.

Many have questioned O'Connor's preoccupation with the sins of upright, decent people. But there's a significant precedent—in the Gospels. Consider the parable of the Pharisee and the Tax Collector:

> Two people went up to the temple to pray; one was a Pharisee and the other was a tax collector.
>
> The Pharisee took up his position and spoke this prayer to himself, "O God, I thank you that I am not like the rest of humanity—greedy, dishonest, adulterous—or even like this tax collector. I fast twice a week, and I pay tithes on my whole income."
>
> But the tax collector stood off at a distance and would not even raise his eyes to heaven but beat his breast and prayed, "O God, be merciful to me, a sinner."

> "I tell you, the latter went home justified, not the former; for everyone who exalts himself will be humbled and the one who humbles himself will be exalted." [Luke 18:10-14]

The parable seems overly harsh on the Pharisee. But that's only because we've forgotten what pride is. Lewis reminds us: Pride is "the essential vice, the utmost evil...it is the complete anti-God state of mind."

Then there's St. Thomas Aquinas: "Pride extinguishes all the virtues and destroys the powers of the soul, since its rule extends to them all."

Pride sets us against each other, and, most importantly, against God. To cure us of it, God allows us to sin. Again, St. Thomas: "The gravity of sins of pride is shown by the fact that God allows man to fall into other sins in order to heal him from pride."

For O'Connor, God's providence was realized not despite our sins, but through them. Removing sin from life—or fiction—meant essentially cutting yourself off from the possibility of grace. Life, or literature, becomes either sentimental or obscene, and while "preferring the former, and being more of an authority on the latter," the Catholic reader fails to see their similarity. "He forgets," she continues, that:

> sentimentality is an excess, a distortion of sentiment usually in the direction of an overemphasis on innocence and that innocence whenever it is overemphasized in the ordinary human condition, tends by some natural law to become its opposite.... Sentimentality is a skipping of this process in its concrete reality and an early arrival at a mock state of innocence, which strongly suggests its opposite.

The opposite of innocence? Abu Ghraib, maybe? When we consider the United States, was there ever a country more naïvely,

optimistically moral? But by separating sin from nature, we forever see ourselves as innocent and exceptional—a chosen people
ordained by God to rid the earth of evil in a War on Terror. Was
there ever a greater occasion for pride? Is this the real meaning of the
Abu Ghraib photographs? Are these images evidence of the subterranean flaw beneath our benevolent, Christian surface?

For Flannery O'Connor, such contradictions explained Southern
literature's tendency toward the violent and grotesque.

> The South is struggling mightily to retain her identity against great
> odds and without knowing always, I believe, quite in what her iden-
> tity lies. An identity is not made from what passes, from slavery to
> segregation, but from those qualities that endure because they are
> related to the truth. It is not made from the mean average or the
> typical but often from the hidden and most extreme.

According to O'Connor, the South was not so much "Christ-
Centered" as "Christ-Haunted." She believed that the most challenging images of Christ were pushed aside in the South in favor of
more palatable ones, ones that would allow for continued separa-
tion and inequality between races. However, these sublimated images eventually return as "fierce and instructive" ghosts to cast
menacing shadows across the landscape. These menacing shadows
are the raw material of much Southern literature, from the well-
mannered Eudora Welty to the drunken, tortured genius of Faulkner.
As Susan Sontag pointed out in her *New York Times Magazine* essay
about Abu Ghraib, "Regarding the Torture of Others," those same
ghosts can be seen in the lynching photos of the late 19th and early
20th century.

And so we see America 2006 also as "Christ-Haunted." Tom
Junod's article "Jesus 2004," which appeared in the May 2004 issue
of *Esquire*, reports that 80 percent of Americans believe in Jesus

Christ and consider themselves Christian. What differs wildly, however, is exactly whom these 80 percent think they're believing in. Junod's piece reveals there is no consensus, but in general Christ is a good guy, he's there for us when we need him, he's personable, even handsome. Ultimately, Junod suggests the personalization of Jesus, the recasting of Jesus in our own (inevitably disordered) human image. This is a phenomenon O'Connor witnessed even in the early sixties. Our concept of Christ has, O'Connor wrote, "gone underneath and come out in distorted forms."

In March 1961, O'Connor received a letter from a professor of English "writing as a spokesman for three members of our department and some ninety university students in three classes" who had been discussing "A Good Man is Hard to Find," her most anthologized and debated story. The plot goes like this: A family of four (Mom, Dad, Sis and Brother) driving along with their self-righteous, superficial, tagalong grandmother, get into an accident on a deserted country road. An escaped convict called "the Misfit" happens on the scene with his gang and proceeds to execute each family member, one by one, in the nearby woods. The grandmother is the last to be killed, but, before she's shot, she tries to save her own life by appealing to the Misfit's belief in God. The letter reads:

> We have debated at length several possible interpretations, none of which fully satisfies us. In general we believe that the appearance of the Misfit is not "real" in the same sense that the incidents of the first half of the story are real. Bailey [the father], we believe, imagines the appearance of the Misfit, whose activities have been called to his attention on the night before the trip and again during the stopover at the roadside restaurant. Bailey, we further believe, identifies himself with the Misfit and so plays two roles in the imaginary last half of the story. But we cannot, after great effort, determine the point at

which reality fades into illusion or reverie. Does the accident literally occur, or is it part of Bailey's dream? Please believe me when I say we are not seeking an easy way out of our difficulty. We admire your story and have examined it with great care, but we are convinced that we are missing something important which you intended us to grasp. We will all be very grateful if you comment on the interpretation which I have outlined above and if you will give us further comments about your intention in writing "A Good Man is Hard to Find."

O'Connor replied, "To a Professor of English":

The interpretation of your ninety students and three teachers is fantastic and about as far from my intentions as it could get to be. If it were a legitimate interpretation, the story would be little more than a trick and its interest would be simply abnormal psychology.

There is a change of tension from the first part of the story to the second where the Misfit enters, but this is no lessening of reality. This story is, of course, not meant to be realistic in the sense it portrays everyday doings of people in Georgia. It is stylized and its conventions are comic even though its meaning is serious.

O'Connor was by then used to comments like this from readers who mistook the Misfit's disavowal of Christianity as just one more reason why the grandmother was sympathetic and good. The Misfit says:

Jesus was the only One who ever raised the dead...and he shouldn't have done it. He thrown everything off balance. If He did what He said, then it's nothing for you to do but throw away everything you own and follow Him, and if He didn't, then it's nothing for you to do but enjoy the few minutes you got left the best way you can—by killing somebody or burning down his house or doing some other meanness to him. No pleasure but meanness.

The English professor's letter misses the point of the Misfit's answer, and the good Christian grandmother's lapse into doubt, as she says, "Maybe He didn't raise the dead." When the Misfit, in a moment of despair, breaks down and says, "If I had of been there I would have known, and I wouldn't be like I am now," the grandmother's eyes are opened and she issues her famous last statement: "Why you're one of my own babies. You're one of my own children." The shock of her words, and her reaching to touch him, causes the Misfit to "spring back as if a snake had bitten him," and then shoot her. Thus the stakes of O'Connor's story are revealed: it's about the question of Christ's authenticity.

That some readers didn't "get" her stories O'Connor blamed on the "Manichean spirit of the times," a spirit which caused a "disjunction between sensibility and belief." This disjunction was at the root of calls for O'Connor to "... express this great country—which is enjoying unparalleled prosperity, which is the strongest nation in the world, and which has produced an almost classless society," instead of writing stories filled with violence and deception.

According to O'Connor this was the fundamental divide between her vision as a Christian writer and what many of her readers expected. These readers wanted to:

> ... separate mystery from manners and judgment from vision, in order to produce something a little more palatable to the modern temper... [and to] form our consciences in the light of statistics, which is to establish the relative as absolute.

O'Connor's "Good Man" is informed by this very tension. Its ending illustrates what happens when these divergent sensibilities converge. When, at the end, the Misfit says of the grandmother, "She would have been a good woman if it had been somebody to shoot her every minute of her life," he's acknowledging that when, on the brink of death, she looked into his face, she saw what Jesus sees in every human being. God's grace is at work here: the Misfit's rage abates, if only briefly, and the grandmother's pride is burned away.

People hounded O'Connor about the meaning of the ending. One letter to O'Connor asks, "Why did you end the story the way you did? Isn't it clear that the reader sympathizes with her?" To which O'Connor replied, "I guess I should have kept writing till the police arrived." Which is to say, "Don't you see? We are a culture obsessed with this kind of ending." O'Connor's artistic vision, her Christ-centered view of the world, makes the old *deus ex machina* obsolete and sentimental—too little too late. Her stories never end with the good being delivered from the evil, with the police arriving to restore order. The most you can hope for in O'Connor's stories is a glimpse of what is, to her, real: that God's love, visible in the ultimate sacrifice of his only begotten son, conquers death— even the fictional kind.

But alas, this usually happens via violence, the only thing that will get her characters'—and the reader's—attention, she famously said.

Will Christians in America see the images of prison abuse at Abu Ghraib as O'Connor would, as evidence of the spiritual struggle within all human beings, or as the Professor of English would, as a deviant fantasy dreamed up by desperate characters? What is the cost of treating these events as the result of abnormal psychology? At what cost do we demand to see ourselves as redeemers—the judgers of Good and Evil?

. . . .

Pictures of the Floating World: On the Occasion of the 60th Anniversary of the Bombing of Hiroshima, in Three Parts

"Excuse me for having no burden like yours."

. . .

The Reverend Mr. Kiyoshi Tanimoto,
quoted in *Hiroshima* by John Hersey

I.

WHEN I WAS IN THE FIFTH GRADE I began going to the library with my dad every Sunday. I remember one particular Sunday browsing the young-adult section in a funky little corner near the LP record listening stations, where homeless men shared headphones and listened to jazz, surrounded by their shopping bags full of clothing. Browsing a spinner rack jammed with books, I came upon a worn-out paperback with the word HIROSHIMA in bold letters across the cover and a photograph of a gigantic mushroom cloud. I doubt that I knew the term "mushroom cloud" then, but I recognized the towering grey cloud from somewhere—TV? A comic book? But to be sure, the word and the image together held no associations for me.

The austerity of the cover made it seem important, as though this one explosion was different from all others. I was about eleven years old and I liked the idea of being able to read young-*adult* books. So I sat down there near the homeless men bopping their heads to Parker and Monk—music for the atomic age—and began reading.

Hersey's prose was direct, focusing on the banal particulars of a morning in Hiroshima, Japan. He wrote with an almost holy reverence for the events of that morning, careful to chronicle the last incredulous moments before the bomb detonated in a flash of molten-hot light. I thought, Where have I been? This event seemed much too important for me to not have known about it.

Never before had I read a book that described the ravages of war so explicitly. The skin of people's hands sloughed off in glove-like pieces, a woman's naked torso was emblazoned with the flowered pattern of the kimono she was wearing when the intense heat and light irradiated her. It was not the complete flattening of the city that unhinged me, but the way the survivors' bodies—the elderly,

47

young mothers and young children—all bore the burns of invisible radiation and tremendous heat.

Never had I read a book shot through with so much guilt. "Excuse me for having no burden like yours," the Reverend Mr. Kiyoshi Tanimoto says to the dazed and bleeding people while hurrying through the smoke and dust-darkened streets, knowing that he can do nothing to save them. I couldn't get my mind around the idea of feeling such deep guilt simply for having lived.

Not long after reading the book I watched a documentary on PBS about the bombing. By this time I had grown obsessed with the event, and I recall even being excited as I sat there on the couch waiting for it to begin. My dad watched it with me, making it seem like a manly thing we were doing, cultivating a deep and thorough knowledge of world events and history. We were probably munching popcorn, something we always do when watching TV. Like Hersey's book, the documentary focused on brutal and heartbreaking eyewitness accounts. The narrator told of a woman and infant lying on the ground near the Hiroshima River. After some time the mother died, but the infant continued to nurse at her breast. An illustration accompanied the narration of this devastating story. Watching the infant crawl up on its mother's limp body, the hair stood up on the back of my neck, and I felt a deep twinge of horror.

An old wrinkled woman, just a teenager when the bomb dropped, told of how her mother had been completely vaporized by the bomb blast as she sat on the steps of the Hiroshima bank waiting for it to open. She held up a photo to the camera: a dark spot on the steps where her mother's body had left a shadow.

II.

ALMOST TWENTY YEARS AFTER MY FIRST READ of *Hiroshima*, on the sixtieth anniversary of the blast, the news coverage I witnessed on the major networks consisted of little more than brief footage of memorial ceremonies in Japan. On NBC there was no mention of the number of Japanese deaths; instead, an interview with a crew member of the Enola Gay, who expressed no regret after over half a century. It felt like a good time to reread Hersey's book, but my copy was missing.

I drove to the library, but their copies were either checked out or missing, so I went looking for the original issue of the *New Yorker*, where the entire book had first been published on August 31, 1946. I went down into the basement where the periodical holdings are squeezed into movable shelves. I cranked back several shelves and walked between the futuristic units, better suited for brushed aluminum cylinders containing double helixes than the faded bindings of magazines like *Canadian Nurse*. I found the correct volume, seven-inches thick, lugged it out of the stacks and sat down at a table. Inside the front cover, written in tight cursive with pencil was a note: Missing volume 22, issue 29. I flipped through the huge fan of brittle musty pages, past ads for hair tonic and phonographs, knowing the missing issue was exactly the one I was looking for. But then there it was: August 31, 1946, a year and twenty-five days after "Little Boy" detonated 580 meters above the center of Hiroshima, killing one hundred and forty thousand people, some vaporized instantaneously. The cover wasn't what I'd expected. It was a colorful painting, an aerial view of hundreds of people basking on blankets in the summer sun of Central Park. Inside I was surprised to see the familiar heading, GOINGS ON ABOUT TOWN, in the same font you'll find in a *New Yorker* now. I love reading through the movie listings and art openings, but my favorite is the jazz column. I always check to see who's playing at the Village Vanguard—it's a dream of mine to see a show at the Vanguard before I die. Now Playing: *The Big Sleep* ("with gun-fire and tough talk"), *Notorious* and *The Postman Always Rings Twice*. Plays: *Harvey*. With Music: Ethel Merman in *Annie Get Your Gun*; *Carousel*; Mr. R and Mr. H's *Oklahoma!*; Buddy Ebsen in *Show Boat;* At the Spotlite: Coleman Hawkins's and Roy Eldridge's bands; Billie Holiday at Downbeat, a place, the writer cautions, resembling a subway car in size.

Surrounding the tiny printed entertainment listings there are ads: Rise and Shine in Randoms by Stetson; The Beau Catcher; Ford V-8 engines; glistening satin stripes ... pale pink or blue on rustling black rayon taffeta. I forgot for a moment what I'd come looking for. I fantasized about what I would give to have seen Billie Holiday in that tiny, smoky club.

Finally I turned the page, eager to set eyes on the original article, as it would have been seen by readers sixty years ago, but what I saw was the cover of the next issue—September 7, 1946. Someone had razored out the entire rest of the issue. All sixty-eight pages of what has been called the greatest magazine article of all time, gone. The reference librarians were sorry: It wasn't available on microfiche. Special Collections didn't have a copy. So I drove over to the small women's college a mile away. There in the basement of the library, I found it:

TO OUR READERS

The *New Yorker* this week devotes its entire editorial space to an article on the almost complete obliteration of a city by one atomic bomb, and what happened to the people of that city. It does so in the conviction that few of us have yet comprehended the all but incredible destructive power of this weapon, and that everyone might well take time to consider the terrible implications of its use.—The Editors

I took a deep breath and read it through, all sixty-eight pages, looking for any differences between it and the book published soon after. The first seven pages are column after column—three to a page—of text. And then the ads start:

"Snooperscope"—sees at night with invisible light! (Below there is an inset picture of a soldier aiming a rifle with a telescopic sight affixed.)

The ad continues:

Here our infrared telescope is mounted on a carbine. The combination was aptly called "sniperscope," for it enabled a soldier in total darkness to hit a target the size of a man at seventy five yards. Thirty percent of the Japanese casualties during the first three weeks of the Okinawa campaign were attributed by the Army to this amazing sniperscope.

Aqua Velva (Men in plaid jackets and derbys at the race track.)
Vat 69 Scotch Whiskey
Perma-lift: The Lift that Never Lets You Down

I finished reading and drove home. As I drove, I found myself thinking more about the ads for Aqua Velva and scotch and how much I would have liked to see Billie Holiday sing in that little jazz club than the fate of the citizens of Hiroshima. I imagined an entire scenario: reeking of Aqua Velva, drinking a scotch, smoking a Camel, I listened to Billie sing her signature tune, "Strange Fruit":

Southern trees bear strange fruit,
Blood on the leaves and blood at the root,
Black bodies swinging in the southern breeze,
Strange fruit hanging from the poplar trees.

Pastoral scene of the gallant south,
The bulging eyes and the twisted mouth,

Scent of magnolias, sweet and fresh,
Then the sudden smell of burning flesh.

Here is fruit for the crows to pluck,
For the rain to gather, for the wind to suck,
For the sun to rot, for the trees to drop,

Here is a strange and bitter crop.

The fantasy blotted Hiroshima from my mind, if only briefly, as I soon remembered the landscape that Miss Sasaki took in almost a month after the blast. It was her first glimpse of the destruction, since she had spent the previous days in a hospital with an infected leg. In Hersey's words:

> Even though the wreckage had been described to her, and though she was still in pain, the sight horrified and amazed her, and there was something she noticed about it that particularly gave her the creeps. Over everything—up through the wreckage of the city, in gutters, along the riverbanks, tangled among tiles and tin roofing, climbing on charred tree trunks—was a blanket of fresh, vivid, lush, optimistic green; the verdancy rose even from the foundations of ruined houses. Weeds already hid the ashes and wild flowers were in bloom among the city's bones. The bomb had not left the underground organs of plants intact; it had stimulated them.

III.

THE SATURDAY AFTER THANKSGIVING, looking at Japanese Ukiyo-e paintings in the Art Institute of Chicago with my friend Brandon, we talk about writing. We read a placard on the wall that explains Ukiyo-e means "pictures of the floating world," although it is alternately translated "sorrowful world." Simple images of snowy mountain passes and young women in scarlet kimonos passing over bridges remind Brandon of William Carlos Williams's mantra: No ideas but in things. Brandon is a poet and he wants to write poetry that is as arresting as these small paintings. The more particulars, the more lived-in a world feels, I tell him, pointing to a tree heavy with snow. The more it seems real, he says. The more possibilities, I say—one image, or perhaps a cluster, causes us to see that the world is vast and mysterious.

I remind him of the previous morning, the red-and-blue box kite we saw stuck way up in a tree on the farm where we, together with my wife, Jessica, cut down a Christmas tree. That is the kind of particular that can make a story, I say. Not by itself, he says. No, not by itself. But the more images like those you have...

On our way back to the city from the Christmas-tree farm, we stopped to gawk at butchered hogs that had been split open and hung like crucifixions on the lawn of a farmhouse. Four hog heads sat in a row in the foreground, staring dumbly at us. Jessica rolled down the window and snapped a picture. For some reason I was nervous, as though this was insensitive, as though the person who did the butchering was going to come out and be upset with us. But when we looked and saw these butchered hogs, the four heads, so perfect in their composition, we saw a picture. Could this be real? A picture was needed for proof, but also because it was strangely beautiful. So that's what a butchered hog looks like—something we knew happened, somewhere, but we gaped at the tableaux like the three naïve city-dwellers we were. The butchered hogs seemed like the still center of the world.

As we drove home, the top of the Christmas tree poking into the front seat by the gear shift, I thought of the day's images: the picture I took of my pregnant wife in front of our first Christmas tree before we cut it down, the kite in the tree, the slaughtered hogs. The images built one on the next, the previous giving way to the most recent. So that what I will remember most about this day—our first Christmas as a married couple—is that picture of the butchered hogs and the nervousness I felt sitting there waiting for Jess to snap the picture. This is not so much irony as it is the beauty of living, each new particular stuns us with its newness, irrevocably changing the complexion of the day, which, I realize, is easy for me to say, living here in Indiana, far from any war zone.

Yoshito Matsushige, a cameraman who took some of the first photos of the aftermath of the Hiroshima blast said upon revisiting the spot where he first encountered injured civilians:

> The children had all suffered burns. Skin was hanging from them like rags. It was cruel to photograph them, and [long pause] at first I couldn't bring myself to do it. I think the first shot took me 30 minutes. The skin was hanging from the children. [I thought,] this is not clothing it's skin.

Such a realization is devastating. Realizing the factuality of the moment: This is real; this is happening right in front of me. Such moments—an infant nursing at a dead mother's breast, four hog heads in a neat row on the side of a country road, children with their skin hanging from their bodies—have the power to obliterate all other circumstances of the day, and those leading up to it.

IV

. . . .

Some Proximity to Darkness

We are all somewhat strangers to our own hearts, and ritual can help us become more acquainted with our hearts, but in ways that are not always pleasant and peaceful. A period of estrangement, of fear and disorientation, is often necessary to effect a true and meaningful examination of our hearts.

. . . .

James Burtchaell, *Philemon's Problem*

ONE MORNING, SURFING THE INTERNET, I ran across an ad for the *Faces of Death* boxed set, an underground gross-out video series popular when I was in middle school.

The ad promised me more than seven hours of "real" explicit footage for just $69.95. For my money, I'd get to watch a bloody pit-bull fight, the clubbing of baby seals, a man immolating himself, an electrocution, San Francisco cannibals chowing down on human organs, a visit to a slaughterhouse, an alligator attack, torture and murder at the hands of guerilla death squads in El Salvador, Napalm bombings in Vietnam, the drugging of a monkey, a dolphin slaughter, a train disaster in India, Cambodian lepers, a wreck on the Autobahn, drug smugglers meeting their demise in Florida's Everglades, a parachutist landing in a crocodile pit, a videotaped rape/murder, a gruesome encounter between a car thief and two junkyard dogs, a cremation, a terrorist destroyed by his own bomb, the massacre of a Columbian wedding party, the drawing and quartering of a Russian peasant and a man-eating tiger turning on its trainer.

The cardboard sleeve that held the videotape read: "When making believe isn't enough."

Immediately I remembered going to a "make-out" party in eighth grade. I was told girls and boys would to be stuck together at the mouth on the stairs, on the couch, in bedrooms and sewing rooms and laundry rooms, under the dining room table, but when I got there the girls were practicing their cheerleading routines on the front lawn, and all the boys were in the basement crowded around the television, laughing at footage of people throwing themselves off buildings or shooting themselves in the head, a monkey being beaten to death with a hammer, autopsy videos, and a hiker being mauled by a bear.

Even then I didn't like the videos. Not that I was morally against them at the age of thirteen; it just wasn't my idea of a good time—a bunch of guys sitting around laughing at horrendous atrocities, saying things like, "That's sick," "Dude, did you see that?" and "Rewind it!" One kid grabbed the VCR remote control and tried to pause the tape right at the moment when the body hit the ground, and then when the bullet entered the suicide's head. It was all but impossible, but this jackass tried anyway.

That afternoon after viewing the ad, as I mowed the grass, I couldn't stop thinking about it, seeing flashes of an anonymous basement surrounded by kids I didn't even like, watching the awful images through a slot in my fingers. What was I thinking? Had they affected my brain?

It was the first time that I'd mowed the yard since my wife and I moved into this new house here in Indiana. It's a chore I hadn't had to mess with in years as I'd been living in apartments in Pittsburgh. Golden light filled the backyard, lighting up the unpainted fence and making even the pale-green weeds along the perimeter look beautiful, like out of a dream of summers past. The light, the smell of gasoline and cut grass, triggered even deeper memories and a more vivid chain of images. This was the same mower that I used to mow the lawns of our neighbors when I was in high school.

Back then, I liked mowing because it gave me time to think. Mostly I thought about movies. I watched a lot of movies. It was the only thing to do besides walking up and down the galleria of Hickory Point Mall and hacking around at Paul's mini golf—only one of the three courses was any good. As I mowed, I saw scenes in my head of those films I watched at fifteen, sixteen. I can't say that I was thinking anything very profound about them, but the scenes were there, clear as crystal. I stared at them, running them forward a bit and then rewinding them back, not in that funny way where you see people moving in reverse, but more like DVD chapters—skipping around from scene to scene, moment to moment, admiring each.

The Godfather is the first film I remembered, particularly the scene where Sonny gets shot up at the toll plaza and the moment where Luca Braisi is choked from behind so that his eyes bulge out his head, and of course the scene where Michael assassinates the crooked police chief who earlier broke his jaw and the Turk, the mobster who is trying to convince the Family to help him sell heroin. I watched *The Godfather* and its sequels more times than I can count in my best friend Joe's basement. It was a ritual we performed every year beginning in seventh grade. Our birthdays are one day apart, so we would have a sleep over, eat spaghetti topped with Francis Ford Coppola's family recipe for marinara that someone had found in a newspaper article, and then stay up all night watching the epic films in the pitch dark. But there was one scene I kept coming back to, one that I couldn't stop thinking about—the scene where Sonny beats up his sister's husband, Carlo, for smacking her around.

Sonny comes in, sees his sister's bruised face and bites his fist in outrage. Out in the street he sees him, Carlo, standing on a stoop in a loud suit. Sonny begins to chase him. An open fire hydrant sprays water in the street. Sonny throws Carlo into some garbage cans and kicks him. Then he picks a can up and tosses it down on top of him. Carlo grabs on to the railing, and when he won't let go Sonny bites his hand. He bites his hand! Why does that one detail stick with me? I was impressed by how angry Sonny was. His actions spoke to me about how a brother might love his sister. Somehow, this wasn't brutality. In the moment when he is biting a man's knuckles and beating him into oblivion in a water-filled gutter, this was love.

A Clockwork Orange was a close second to *The Godfather*. The scene in which Alex is strapped down and forced to watch images of violence and rape was not lost on me. Alex was, in a subterranean way, like me—fascinated by sex and violence, and a little confused as to where one ended and the other began. *A Clockwork Orange* was a way for me to get some glimpses of nudity and violence that I knew could be found in pornography, without the guilt. I liked telling people I'd seen *A Clockwork Orange*, especially the older kids at school whom I wanted to impress. It was a way to seem cool, unbothered by violence. I felt one notch cooler than before I'd seen it.

There's a Leonard Michaels story that I like to teach my young fiction-writing students titled "Murderers" in which the narrator, a man looking back on the death of his uncle, describes how after the death—a heart attack—he needed "some proximity to darkness, strangeness." "Who doesn't," he asks rhetorically. So he rides the subways all day long from Queens to Coney Island brooding, thinking deeply about himself and his place in the world because he "didn't want to wait for it"—his own death.

Joe's basement was our subway, the place we went for darkness, strangeness and a good old derangement of the senses without the aid of drugs or alcohol. We could watch anything we wanted pretty much undisturbed, and when I left his basement at the end of the night and walked out to the curb where my dad was waiting in our van, bleary-eyed, listening to WLS talk radio out of Chicago, a program where a conservative host named "Mad Dog" Bob Lassiter would berate his guests, I often didn't know how to explain what I'd seen. In fact, what I'd seen was usually not something I could discuss in terms of plot, but only in sounds, sensations and images.

Then one night, I believe we were freshman in high school, we watched David Lynch's *Blue Velvet*. Things were different after that.

Early in the film Jeffrey, a naïve college boy, finds a severed ear in a vacant lot. The camera closes in on the ear, gradually extending its gaze down into the canal until we are spiraling through a portal, crossing a threshold to another reality. The gesture recalls Lynch's *Eraserhead*, in which the viewer passes a Promethean gatekeeper to a gritty, black, urban landscape where industrial white noise drones in the background. But in *Blue Velvet*, we pass through to a world that looks no different than the one we left; in fact, no different than the one I lived in, in central Illinois. On the surface are lush lawns, white picket fences and beautiful tree-lined streets. But Jeffrey's curiosity, his determination to solve the mystery of the severed ear, leads him beneath this pristine surface to the apartment of lounge singer Dorothy Vallens where, while hiding in a closet, he witnesses fetishistic sex and learns that beneath the polished surface of Lumberton are kidnapping, blackmail, sexual deviance and all-around degeneracy, embodied in the supremely disturbed underworld kingpin Frank Booth.

Within this detective story is a coming-of-age love story involving Jeffrey and Sandy, the police chief's daughter. Sandy is both intrigued and disturbed by Jeffrey's obsession with the case, remarking at one point, "I don't know whether you're a detective or a pervert." I liked the idea of being both, not having to choose. I figured it could make you a better detective.

Jeffrey was the kind of hero I fancied myself—naïve and unassuming, yet capable of ultimately prevailing over the darkness. He says, "There are opportunities in life for gaining knowledge and experience. Sometimes it's necessary to take a risk." Amen, I thought.

I was naïve to what I was actually saying Amen to. Lynch said of the film in an interview:

I'd always had a desire to sneak into a girl's apartment and watch her through the night. I had the idea that while I was doing this I'd see something which I'd later realize was the clue to a mystery. I think people are fascinated by that, by being able to see into a world they couldn't visit. That's the fantastic thing about cinema, everybody can be a voyeur. Voyeurism is a bit like watching television—go one step further and you want to start looking in on things that are really happening.

Blue Velvet is a film that considers the co-existence, rather than the mutual exclusivity, of good and evil in the heart of the country, with Jeffrey as the "only bridge between the two," according to Lynch. But I was blind to this fact—that Blue Velvet was about the desire to be a voyeur, that the film implicated me, rather than giving me a license to righteously point and laugh at the freaks.

Novelist J.G. Ballard wrote in his review of Blue Velvet that the film was like "The Wizard of Oz reshot with a script by Kafka and décor by Francis Bacon." Like Oz, Lynch's films begin in a recognizable place, but the action takes us beneath the surface to places that seem on the outer rim of reality—hellish, downright evil places, where language breaks down (recall the backwards-speaking midget in Twin Peaks), identity is shattered (Bill Pullman and Balthazar Ghetty trade identities in Lost Highway), and where time and logic are distended. Whether urban or rural, Lynch's characters are naïve and genuinely surprised by the darkness they confront—many times inside of themselves. His vision is moralistic, showing us the downward spiral—the disappointment, delusion, and self-doubt— that sex and violence can cause. There is something of Greek tragedy at work in his films: enterprise and indomitable curiosity lead his heroes on quests to find their identity, sometimes literally, as in Lost Highway and Mulholland Drive. It's an ancient theme, even a cliché; but, Lynch points out, we continue to see ourselves reflected in it.

This was the kind of darkness and strangeness I wanted, something that wasn't just obscene, but rather something surreal, mysterious and impenetrable, something that would stick with me for a while, like the parables I grew up hearing at Mass, which did not yield their meaning all at once, but seemed to reveal more and more of their truth each year.

In one of the most disturbing scenes in *Blue Velvet*, Dorothy appears, naked and in shock, walking unsteadily down the middle of Jeffrey's street—a nod, some have suggested, to the famous Vietnam war photo of a young girl running, naked and crying, toward the camera. Years later, reading an interview with Lynch, I learned that this image was taken from his youth. An emotionally disturbed neighbor had done something similar. He wasn't trying to be strange and elusive; he actually thought and saw in these terms. The traumatic images and impulses of his childhood were his inspiration.

In turn, Lynch encouraged me to investigate my own life in this way, looking for those singular moments of contact with mystery. But I wouldn't think of it in those terms for some time to come.

Back then, the mere fact that I wasn't repulsed by what I saw, that I could stomach it and even, at times, laugh, seemed a virtue. I felt a surge of self-importance while watching—*I'm the only one that gets this*. This sort of logic crosses my mind even today. When I finished *The Brothers Karamazov*, watched every single episode of *Twin Peaks* in a week while sick with the flu, saw Francis Bacon's "Figure with Meat" for the sixth or seventh time at the Art Institute of Chicago, I sensed something old passing away and something new taking shape within me: not knowledge or wisdom, but pride for having sought out the most challenging experiences, choosing to subject myself to them, so I could say that I'd gone there, seen it and come back to tell about it.

As I pushed the mower around my small back yard, all these images flashed through my brain, sending me to a kind of examination room within myself, allowing me to take stock of the things I have seen and decide whether they really made me more alive to the world, or more dead.

. . . .

I WENT TO COLLEGE AT THE UNIVERSITY OF NOTRE DAME, located just outside of South Bend, Indiana, ninety miles due east of Chicago, five miles south of the Michigan state line. It's not what you'd call the most culturally happening campus. The last several years, the university has been rated as the least welcoming in the country when it comes to "alternative" life styles—never mind the fact that for most eighteen-year-olds in the U.S. being seriously Catholic is an alternative, even alien, life style. More than eighty percent of the students are Catholic, and for a majority of those students Notre Dame is their first-choice school. It leads all Catholic universities in the number of chapels on campus and in the percentage of students who attend Mass regularly. My dorm mates and I went to Mass together every Sunday night and shook hands and hugged and offered each other the sign of peace.

It's a pristine, mythic place, Notre Dame, a bubble that seems to shield its occupants from all the evil of the outside world. But nothing could keep out Quentin Tarantino's *Pulp Fiction*. It was more violent than anything I'd seen in Joe's basement. More violent than Sonny's death at the tollbooth, more violent than anything dished out by Alex and his droogs.

From the way the upperclassmen who lived in the quad next door described it, it didn't seem to be a movie about anything. It was just a long string of guess-you-had-to-be-there events: the robbery of a diner by a guy named Pumpkin and a women named Honey Bunny, a dance contest, a conversation about what the French call a Quarterpounder with Cheese, did you know you can order a beer at McDonald's in Paris, a debate over foot massage techniques, some verses from the book of the prophet Ezekiel.

It sounded like one big incoherent mess. But the movie was like some sort of coolness carwash: You went in one side a white, nerdy, Catholic-school kid and came out the other hip. *Pulp Fiction*'s language sounded cool in anyone's mouth.

Shit yeah Negro, that's all you had to say!

My section mates and I decided we had to see this movie or risk social ostracization. So six of us piled into a borrowed car and drove across town to the little six-screen theater behind the Olive Garden.

Inside the dark theater, my retinas were scorched by images of cool, sedate, even casual violence.

I love you Pumpkin.

I love you Honey Bunny.

Any of you fuckin' pricks move and I'll execute every mother-fuckin' last one of you.

Despite the constant barrage of the F-bomb and the N-word, I was carried along by the rhythm of the speech and the slick, sexy, infectious thug mentality, an understanding that all bets were off; the law of the modern jungle was at hand—and it struck me as hysterical. Why?

Anthony Lane, in his *New Yorker* review of *Pulp Fiction*, summed it up by quoting pulp writer Raymond Chandler: "It is not funny that a man should be killed, but it is sometimes funny that he should be killed for so little, and that his death should be the coin of what we call civilization."

Cases in point:

Marsellus Wallace throwing Antwan Rockamora, one of his associates, off a balcony and through a glass greenhouse for giving Marsellus's wife, Mia, a foot massage.

Marvin, a lackey of Jules and Vincent, has his brains "accidentally" splattered all over the interior of Vincent's car when the car hits a bump causing Vincent's gun to go off.

The instances of violence are isolated, out of context, due to the cut-up chronology of Tarantino's plot, and therefore seem to stand on their own, as gags, free of hard feelings or consequences. *Pulp Fiction*'s mixed-up narrative creates the impression that there are no serious ramifications to the character's actions. Tarantino's experiment breaks new ground, proving that violence is funnier in the absence of consequences, especially when it is committed by ridiculous-looking thugs—Vincent sports a greasy mullet, Jules a classic Jheri Curl.

The inane humor of *Pulp Fiction*—serious conversations about foot massages seconds before committing triple murder—insulated (inoculated?) us from the violence. The actions are reprehensible, but the dialogue is full of inconsequential, trivial bullshit— where to get a good hamburger, taking a moment to savor a sip of gourmet coffee while a headless corpse bleeds in your car.

The humor precludes any deeper meaning. Few moviegoers seriously contemplate the meaning of the passage from Ezekiel: "the righteous man is beset on all sides" by the "iniquity of evil men." No one *really* considers why Butch goes back to save Marsellus Wallace from being raped and almost certainly killed by "hillbilly rapists," or why a beautiful and charming woman like Mia would want to marry a murderous thug like Marsellus Wallace in the first place.

Why? Because nobody is interested in *why*. The movie doesn't invite any of these questions.

No one believes that Jules has witnessed a miracle—that God came down and stopped the bullets—but it's fun to hear him rationalize it because it's fun to hear Samuel L. Jackson talk.

God came down and stopped those motherfuckin' bullets.

I see the scenes playing as surely now, on this sunny afternoon, eleven years later, as I could then, just minutes afterwards, wedged in the back seat of that borrowed car, driving back to campus, already trying to perfect our Samuel L. Jackson impressions.

I don't remember asking you a goddamn thing!

Lynch's moralistic view of violence mixed with Tarantino's, so that even though I was waking up to the fact that there was an entire world of darkness and sin out there, it was situated far from Notre Dame, out there in the riotous inner-city of LA and the Midwestern wastelands: East St. Louis; the projects of Chicago; Gary, Indiana; places I had only seen from a moving car. It seemed that the evil and degradation of the outside world was kept at bay, at the edges of campus, where trash gathered in the gutters, cars rusted in vacant lots and people were unhappy with their lives. Meanwhile, inside the bubble, we danced the Macarena in our cramped dorm rooms while Brother Ed, the rector, weeded the flowerbeds out front in his gardening smock, humming contentedly.

I was in the marching band. I paid for my books with checks with scenes from *Star Wars* on them. Instead of the obligatory collection of liquor bottles on my dorm windowsill, I had an army of Pez candy dispensers that my mother sent me in weekly care packages, along with *Star Wars* neckties and Ramen Noodles. After seeing *Pulp Fiction*, I put the Pez dispensers in a desk drawer, bought the screenplay and sat in my room and memorized it, studying what was cool.

Every party we went to, the *Pulp Fiction* soundtrack played and people danced like Travolta and Thurman at the Jackrabbit Slim's twist contest. In dining-hall conversations we raved over Mia Wallace being stabbed in her cleavage with a hypodermic needle full of Adrenalin; Christopher Walken's tour-de-force monologue about war buddies hiding heirloom watches up their ass; the emergence of the leather-masked Gimp from his holding cell and Samuel L. Jackson's grand inquisition of Brett, the failed preppy drug dealer:

> "What country you from?!"
> "What?"
> "What ain't no country I ever heard of. Do they speak English in What?"

But no one said much about Zed, an LA County Sheriff, sodomizing a black underworld gangster. Not even Anthony Lane of the *New Yorker* mentioned it.

It's probably the most disturbing and graphically violent moment in all of *Pulp Fiction*. Butch pushes open the door to the basement room and we see Zed raping Marsellus Wallace. It was simply not talked about in any depth other than the "wrongness" of it, as in "that's just wrong."

Both Wallace and Butch are tough, loud-mouthed men, a gangster and a boxer, but bound and gagged in the dank basement of the pawnshop they lose their voices and become powerless. So too is "The Gimp," a man in a full leather bondage suit—his entire head and face are completely covered, including his mouth represented by a closed zipper—who is pulled from a box and told to look after Butch while the two men rape Wallace. When I first saw the film with my dorm mates back in 1994, the moment the

Gimp is pulled from the box the entire audience broke into nervous laughter.

Butch is played by Bruce Willis, an actor whose tough-guy star power, carried over from the *Die Hard* movies, seems to preclude him from being raped. In a kind of *Six Million Dollar Man* slo-motion effort, he pulls his hands loose from the ropes binding his hands, punches out the leather-clad Gimp and limps out of the basement. He could escape; however, when he gets upstairs, Butch can still hear the "hillbilly rapists" whooping and grunting over the growling tenor sax soundtrack.

While Marsellus Wallace is raped, we hear only the bawdy, aggressive caricature of Cowboys and Indians—"Comanche"—coming from a radio in the basement. Here, the music does the work of the foul language elsewhere, adding a layer of irony or self-aware cool to the moment, like having sex to Miles Davis's *Kind of Blue* or working out to "We Are the Champions." In Michael Moore's *Bowling for Columbine*, we hear American soldiers in Iraq discussing the specific type of music they listen to while in combat. One solidier describes how he plugs a portable CD player into the communication system of the tank so he can hear the music in his headset. The song? *The roof. The roof. The roof is on fire. We don't need no water let the motherfucker burn. Burn motherfucker burn.* Raping someone to a soundtrack, as Tarantino does, is the ultimate aestheticization of violence.

For reasons that are never made clear, Butch has a change of heart and returns to the basement with a samurai sword to save Marsellus's life, the man who an hour or so before wanted him dead. We see the door from Butch's point of view. We see his hand push it open and the music gets louder, emanating, it seems, from a boom box in the room. Finally we see the long-anticipated act being committed in the dark corner. No more laughter in the theater, just stunned silence.

Up to this point in the film, the violence is quick and surprising; it doesn't interrupt the swaggering rhythm of the dialogue or the jarring pace of the plot. There's a lot of telling, a lot of stories being told, a lot of B.S. being talked. But the rape of Wallace brings the film to a halt. Tarantino chose not to insinuate this moment, but to show it full on.

Years later, watching the film with my dad late one night on cable, I found myself growing very nervous as the moment in question approached. When Butch pushes open the door to reveal the rape, my dad groaned in disgust. I actually thought he might get up and leave the room. Seeing the scene with my father was like seeing it for the first time. Repeat viewings with my friends had inured me to the horror of the act. Over time, "Comanche" had come to remind me of numerous things—dorm parties, ex-girlfriends, shotgunning beers. But seeing it with my dad, all that was stripped away, and I realized how the music had distanced me from the image on the screen.

It's not the first film to set violence to music. Wagner's "Ride of the Valkyrie" accompanies the helicopter assault of a beachhead in *Apocalypse Now*. Old Alex commits the ultraviolent while sinisterly crooning "Singing in the Rain."

Music, like certain drugs and alcohol, lowers our inhibitions and aestheticizes our perception, sensually charging our world so that it appears more beautiful, more heroic, more profound, more despairing. This is no revelation. Consider the strict prohibitions the Third Reich placed on jazz: songs could not exceed a certain metronomic speed (excessively fast tunes, what jazz musicians sometimes called "barn burners," were thought to incite riot and rebellion), and saxophones were to be replaced by violins or violas because saxes were guttural and tribal sounding, therefore appealing to an audience's base emotions.

Music might just be one of the most neglected components to understanding modern attitudes toward images of death and violence. Sure, it always made people drive a little faster, feel more sensual, dance in front of bathroom mirrors like they were rock stars, but the problem here is that when music and images become linked—as in music videos, big-budget Hollywood war films and action flicks, pornography, TV commercials and video games—the human being becomes merely a body in motion, perhaps the most titillating image known to man.

Watching *Pulp Fiction* with my dad, I sensed that there was something deeply wrong at the core of the scene. I began questioning why on earth it ever seemed anything less than horrific to me. Then a thought hit me: What if Marsellus Wallace was not gagged during his rape? What would have come out of his mouth? What if someone turned down the blaring chainsaw sax solo so we could hear what was going on in that room? Would we hear him curse Zed and Maynard? Would he yell "stop"? Would he call for help? Would we see his rape differently now that we could hear him scream? The drowning out of the human voice creates complicity in us—because Marsellus can't cry out in anguish and pain, the consequences seem to be lessened—and we, like Butch, are sworn to the same vow of secrecy, to pretend that this never happened.

This revelation took me back once more to Joe's basement, where I had first seen the film *Deliverance*. I recalled the feeling of violation and sympathy I had for Bobby Trippe, who is also raped, oddly enough, by "hillbillies." It remains unmatched in American film for its ability to make men groan and turn away from the screen. I remember watching the film with the expectation that the scene would be funny. My uncles and my friend's older brothers would sometimes joke, "Boy, you shore got a purdy mouth" and "squeal like a piggy," and laugh hysterically. I laughed too, wanting so badly to fit in and be cool. On its own, by itself, that *is* funny—asking a grown man to squeal like a pig. But within this movie about men reliving their youth, trying to prove that they're still as rugged and virile as when they were teenagers, Bobby Trippe's rape is chilling, especially given the utter silence surrounding the moment. Unlike *Pulp Fiction,* there is no soundtrack to stylize the brutality, allowing us to instead be imprinted with the bald image of sexual brutality. This must have been my first exposure to the pain that rape can cause, not just the physical, but the mental anguish. I could see that this act destroyed Bobby Trippe.

In the film, the scene lasts only a few minutes, whereas in the book, narrated in the first-person, the whole episode lasts for nearly thirty pages.

> The blood was running down from under my jaw where the point [of the knife] had been. I had never felt such brutality and carelessness of touch, or such disregard for another person's body. It was not the steel or the edge of the steel that was frightening; the man's fingernail, used in any gesture of his, would have been just as brutal; the knife only magnified his unconcern. I shook my head again, trying to get my breath in a gray void full of leaves. I looked straight up into the branches of the sapling I was tied to, and then down into the clearing at Bobby.
>
> He was watching me with his mouth open as I gasped for enough breath to live on from second to second. There was nothing he could do, but as he looked at the blood on my chest and under my throat, I could see that his position terrified him more than mine did; the fact that he was not tied mattered in some way.

They both went toward Bobby, the lean man with the gun this time. The white-bearded one took him by the shoulders and turned him around toward downstream.

"Now let's you just drop them pants," he said.

Bobby lowered his hands hesitantly. "Drop . . . ?" he began.

My rectum and intestines contracted. Lord God.

The toothless man put the barrels of the shotgun under Bobby's right ear and shoved a little. "Just take 'em right on off," he said.

"I mean, what's this all . . ." Bobby started again weakly.

"Don't say nothing," the older man said. "Just do it."

The man gave the gun a vicious shove, so quick that I thought the gun had gone off. Bobby unbuckled his belt and unbuttoned his pants. He took them off, looking around ridiculously for a place to put them.

"Them panties too," the man with the belly said.

Bobby took off his shorts like a boy undressing for the first time in a gym, and stood there plump and pink, his hairless thighs shaking, his legs close together.

"See that log? Walk over yonder."

Wincing from the feet, Bobby went slowly over to a big fallen tree and stood near it with his head bowed.

"Now git on down crost it."

The tall man followed Bobby's head down with the gun as Bobby knelt over the log.

And then:

A scream hit me, and I would have thought it was mine except for the lack of breath. It was the sound of pain and outrage, and was followed by one of simple and wordless pain and outrage, and was followed by one of simple and wordless pain. Again it came out of

> him, higher and more carrying. I let all the breath out of myself and
> brought my head down to look at the river.

Once the men are finished with Bobby, they turn to the narrator:

> The two of them turned to me. I drew up as straight as I could and
> waited with the tree. It was up to them. I could . . . see the blood ves-
> sels in the eyes of the tall man. That was all; I was blank.

Dickey's book forces us to meditate on the ugliness of violence through images that are not neutral and objective but that call attention to the way violence, as Simone Weil argues in her revolutionary essay on *The Iliad*, can make a human being into an object. When the narrator reflects, "I had never felt such brutality and carelessness of touch, or such disregard for another person's body," we gain more insight into the mind of the victimized. We learn that the knife is not the focus of the narrator's fear, but rather the man's "unconcern," which the knife "magnifies."

Flannery O'Connor talks of language that is "unlike itself," new and vibrant, vibrating at a frequency producing a pitch that is foreign and haunting, bringing us to states of contemplation and reflection on the violence humans do to other humans—language like a primal scream. Dickey captures such language. Through the carefully chosen and placed word, he is able to capture the spiritual dimension of witnessing. The narrator's observation of Bobby "looking around ridiculously" for a place to neatly lay his pants, the simile which transforms Bobby into a schoolboy "undressing for the first time in a gym," brings me as close to the experience as possible. Dickey captures the language of empathy that compels us to see the violence as despicable, not funny. He also captures the private language of a human being yearning, however irrationally, toward the divine for help—"Lord God," he says, as he watches the moment painfully unfold. There is no way to flinch, to turn away, or close our eyes to it; there is no soundtrack to dull the senses. In silence we witness the transformation (disintegration?) of the innocent into the violated.

After Bobby's rape, the narrator observes something profound of Bobby: "...he was furiously closed off from all of us"—a reaction that speaks directly to the nature of film violence. The pain is closed off from us, compartmentalized within a series of frames. Once it passes we can be shut of it. There is no urge to go back and examine it more closely. As long as the villain is punished and the hero is rewarded the violence seems "just." Pain, injury and even death are rationalized as simply the "cost" of breaking the law or committing an evil act. Marsellus Wallace's rape, according to the morality of the film, is deserved. Bobby's rape is not. But both are regarded as persons to be seen, not persons (like us) who also see and feel— they are fictions. And this fact allows for the brutality to strike many as funny, even slapstick.

Because the characters in *Pulp Fiction*, like most pulp fictions, are never allowed or afforded the ability to speak deeply, originally or meaningfully about the pain they have endured or are enduring, they seem indifferent to the violence they commit and witness. Jules's desire to leave behind thug life after witnessing what he thinks is a miracle is funny to Vincent and to the viewer. It seems like a put-on. It's hard to take seriously a moment of a deep spiritual awakening in the midst of this world where Coolness, unflinching in the face of brutality, is next to Godliness. Grace makes an appearance, but as the motorcycle that carries Butch away from the scene of Marsellus's rape—the word is literally airbrushed on the gas tank of Zed's chopper. Grace in *Pulp Fiction* is no more than a winking *deus ex machina*, not a revelation, just another conventional escape from danger.

In a film seemingly about changing the direction of your life, steering it back on the path of righteousness, Wallace is the one character who maintains his old ways. After Butch saves him from certain death at the hands of his rapists, Wallace shoots Zed in the groin with a shot gun and says, "I'm gonna get me a couple of hard, pipe-hittin' niggas to go to work on homes here...I'm gonna get medieval on your ass." Violence begets violence begets violence. In *Pulp Fiction*, it looks like justice. We approve. Sitting in that theater, eating lunch in the dining hall, we fantasized that we would do the same thing.

Just as Jules rethinks his calling-card Bible passage—"I thought that was just some cold-blooded shit to say to somebody before I put a cap in their ass"—I now realize that the language of *Pulp Fiction* sounds good in anyone's mouth, but is ultimately destructive. It gives us the vocabulary to drown out the screams, to dismiss what we've seen, because it denies the seriousness of the violence—it's just a way to blow off steam, some crazy shit that happened at the office, things got a little out of hand but they deserved it anyway.

Since I first saw the Abu Ghraib photos, I've been cataloguing the images of violence that launched my imagination, hunting a scapegoat, the event that would answer all my questions as to why I am this way.

Even though a photograph is still (according to Sontag) merely "a trace of something brought before the lens," we trust it to tell the truth more vividly than a carefully-researched article. However, the reaction to the Abu Ghraib photographs show us a different tendency, to acknowledge that the images are horrific but to excuse the actions as stemming from circumstances not visible in the photographs, beyond the range of the camera lens. The images seem to show Iraqi detainees being abused and humiliated by American soldiers. But the terms "abuse" and "humiliation" are a matter of one's subjectivity—we must ask whether or not we care that these detainees are being mistreated. We silently assess whether or not we feel that the treatment of these detainees is deserved. The terms "abuse" and "humiliation" hold no currency. And even if they do, the affective currency is judged to be less severe than the gruesome beheadings of American citizens, also captured on video. The pain of these detainees, the majority of who were not insurgents but, at worst, common criminals accused of domestic crimes, is seen as vindication, payback for the pain inflicted on fellow Americans.

In this way, many Americans agree with Donald Rumsfeld's assessment of the situation: "Those pictures never should have gotten out," suggesting that before they were contained some place, locked away, never to be seen. We say the same of gossip—keep it quiet; it's between us. And we also now say the same thing of the tortured person. Once they've been subjected to this treatment they can never really be let out—the truth of what happened to him or her will remain in that room forever, no amount of disclosure of memos or transparency of the detainment process can free the tortured person. Thus we can conclude that not only do the abusive acts shown in the the Abu Ghraib photos rob the detainees of humanity, but they actually embody the process of negation found in pornography, objectifying the photographed for one's own gain.

"The very content of pain is itself negation," writes Elaine Scarry. Pain destroys language, such that the person is negated and the world surrounding them is slowly "unmade," discounted. If we think of the photos and images of the violated and tortured in this way, as memorializing the negation of humanity and the incremental undoing of the world, then we are closer to understanding the stakes of bearing witness. There is no closure when we look away, only unremitting pain and anguish.

GROWING UP, I WAS DRAWN TO DARKNESS, believing it held the
key to understanding. But understanding what? I didn't know. In
Blue Velvet, Jeffrey felt he had to venture down into the darkness
in order to know the world. Darkness and knowledge—there seemed
to be no difference between the two. I criticized the naïvely good
and hated the righteous. I abhorred violence in the abstract, yet
found beauty in images of decay, dissolution and decadence, hoping they'd reveal the Wizard behind the curtain.

My time below ground in Joe's basement put me in touch with
something larger than myself, or so I thought—something awesome. I thought I could see through the darkness. Images of violence can do that, they can startle us anew. They can open up
passages to other realms of understanding: deeper knowledge of
human suffering and cruelty, perhaps even empathy for our enemies. But after all those movies, what had I really seen? Just more
darkness. Violence turns both the perpetrator, the victim and the
witness to stone.

I used to think that Lynch's dark, surreal vision had shaped me
in virtuous ways. I became an elitist, able to see the flaws beneath
Main Street USA. But the import of his films is less self-righteous.
If they can instill virtue, it is because they make visible the grotesque
transformation ordinary people undergo when they are touched
by violence.

The severed ear in the vacant lot invites us to enter, with Jeffrey,
the underworld. We think we'll return uncorrupted, even wiser.
But violence doesn't enlighten; it taints. We can't be both pervert
and detective. We may attain knowledge—power—but not without
compromising our souls.

Now, Lynch's severed ear brings me to the severed ear in the
Gospel of Luke. A disciple strikes the high priest's servant—one of
the many who comes to the garden to capture and crucify Jesus—

cutting off his right ear. Jesus says in reply: "Stop! No more of this."
Then he touches the servant's ear and heals him.

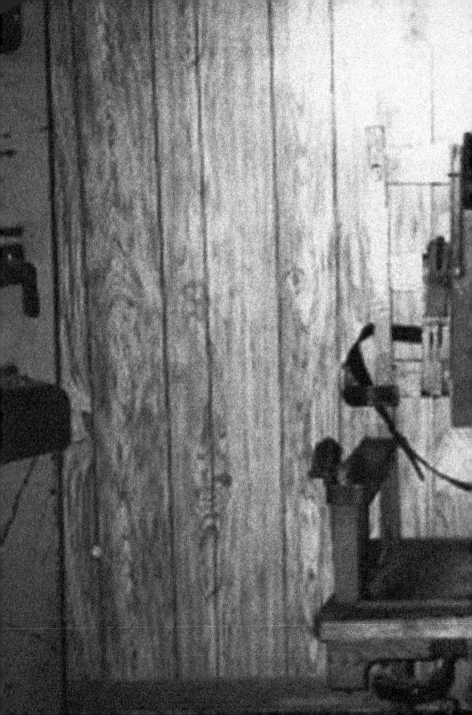

V

. . . .

Regarding the Electric Chair
My Wife's College Boyfriend
Built in His House

WHEN MY WIFE WAS IN COLLEGE IN LOUISIANA she dated a guy who built an electric chair in his house. Made of two-by-fours and copper wire, he and his buddies liked to get drunk and see who could take the most current. Sometimes my wife would sit on it, as I imagine it, a precious look of giddy terror on her face, as with the long ascendancy of a roller coaster, but the instant she would hear the hum of the current and feel the vibration in the wooden arms she would scream, jump from the chair, half-laughing, half-crying, calling the boys retarded.

But, really, she liked it.

They imagined it as something straight out of Andy Warhol's Factory—young, good looking, fashionable people sitting around smoking cigarettes, popping pills, not so much daring one another as clamoring to abuse themselves in some new, exciting way.

This boyfriend of hers loved Warhol and Bret Easton Ellis; he wore oxblood penny loafers and khaki pants and white oxford shirts with the cuffs rolled up. He taught her about fashion and etiquette and indie rock. She was impressionable—an awkward Catholic girl from Slidell, Louisiana, just across Lake Ponchartrain from New Orleans, who grew up reading *Sweet Valley High* and V.C. Andrews's books about incestuous relationships between brothers and sisters, and later anything Anne Rice—real trash, she admits.

This boyfriend was, of course, older. He played in a band and recorded music on a four track in a little home studio in the house they shared, a house that was just down the street from the one used in the film *Sex, Lies, and Videotape.*

The guy had a gun, too, a .357 Magnum. She fired it once. They were down on the bayou, drinking and carrying on: "It's a wonder someone wasn't killed," she says. "It's a good thing I met you."

I don't like thinking of my wife in any makeshift electric chair, or drinking Abita (the local Budweiser-tasting beer), smoking cigarettes and shooting guns on a brackish, humid Louisiana bayou with some dandy. But when she tells these stories I can't help but feel a little prissy, a little less of a man.

I hate pain. I've never been in a fistfight. As a kid, whenever I did get mad enough to fight someone I would start to cry. The only gun I've ever fired is my dad's .22, and it has sat completely disassembled in several slick black pieces atop the book case in the living room of my parents' house for at least fifteen years. I told my wife, "The first time I shot my dad's .22, I was so scared my heart nearly stopped." She laughs, "That's so sad. That's why I love you."

It's comforting to hear that, but then again there's something that sticks in me, there's a barb in her laugh, something down inside of me flinches and rebels. It's like saying, "I love you because you're so weak and ineffectual." I feel like Hemingway's Francis Macomber.

This is not what most men want to hear. Then again, this is what I've wanted to hear all my life. When I was wrestling in the 112-pound weight class my freshman year of high school, listening to Sting's *The Soul Cages* and the Smiths' *Meat is Murder* on my walkman slumped in the bleachers of some rural high school, waiting for my match, I was secretly praying to the good Lord that some girl would love me for my sensitivity. I just couldn't get mad enough to wrestle, to go out there and utterly intimidate and dominate another human being.

Coach Nailes used to try to psych me up before each match by saying, "Come on, Griffith. Get mad!" I wanted to laugh. I won a single match that season—the only season I was to wrestle—and that was by forfeit. The other team didn't have a 112-pound wrestler; he was sick. My teammates cheered loudly, if ironically. When my friends heard about it they howled. I'm pretty proud of that one win. It shows what can happen if you just show up.

I did a lot of thinking that winter, riding around in the back of that sawed off bus—we used the "short bus" most of the time because our team was so small. And one of the things I remember thinking about was how different I was from the people I wrestled, how dedicated and determined and utterly pumped they were to beat my ass and how uninterested I was. This isn't to say that I was some kind of Gandhi of Midwestern high school wrestling, but even then, physical violence repulsed me.

A year later, my interest in sensitivity was vindicated by *The Great Gatsby*, the first book I ever loved: "In my younger years my father gave me some advice that I've been turning over in mind ever since. 'Whenever you feel like criticizing anyone,' he told me, 'just remember that all the people in this world haven't had the advantages you've had.'"

My own father has never, and would never, say such a thing, but still I took it as sound advice. I credit this advice with what my wife calls my great "patience" and what my mother has called my "tolerance," as in, "I think you're too tolerant." And she's right. I've tended in my life to give most people the benefit of the doubt, to withhold my judgment until I've known them long enough to make an educated decision about whether they're good or not. In the process, I've given sympathy to people who deserved a kick in the teeth, and I count myself in that number. As a result I've surrendered what I now understand is considerable moral ground. As Jay Gatsby puts it:

> In consequence I'm inclined to reserve all judgments, a habit that has opened up many curious natures to me and also made me the victim of not a few veteran bores.... Reserving judgments is a matter of infinite hope. I am still a little afraid of missing something if I forget that, as my father snobbishly suggested and I snobbishly

repeat, a sense of the fundamental decencies is parceled out un-
equally at birth.

Ditto. Four times I've been asked for love advice by complete
strangers: once on a long cross-country flight, once in line at the
grocery store, once in a physician's waiting room, and once on the
observation deck of the Sears Tower. I like being friendly, but my
problem has been and continues to be that I don't know where to
draw the line; no topic is too far afield, no action beyond redemption. I'm curious about people, what can I say? I want to hear their
stories, what they've done that morning, who they're waiting on a
call from, when they get paid next.

It's a disease, and I think it was brought on by *The Great Gatsby*.
It was the first book whose narrator spoke in a voice that endeared
him to me, made me believe that he could tell the story and tell it
better than anyone else. This is the job of a narrator, to tell the story
the best he can, making sense of the complicated events and per-
sonalities, the tangled motives and personal relationships, in such
a humane and insightful way as to make us believe that they were
there and now feel compelled to report back to us, not to brag, but
to make us understand the importance of what they have seen. I
know, young people latch on to books with strong, idiosyncratic
narrators. But Nick Carraway is a different animal altogether: not
merely genteel but sensible, not naïve but looking for the good in
people, not charming so much as patient. He's not like the others;
at least that's what I've been telling myself.

Nick Carraway seems to be the conscientious objector of narrators—he has the wherewithal to stay above the fray. He is not drawn
down into the decadence, although he is irrevocably changed by his
experiences with Gatsby. It seems that Nick lives only to record the
flimsy motives, poorly hidden marital strife, bad manners, affairs,

broken noses, hot summer afternoons drinking in stifling hotel rooms, ash heaps, disconcerting billboards and hit-and-runs. He spends little time telling us of his job, his life, his aspirations, a quality I appreciate.

This is why I wanted to be a writer. I felt I could best make sense of the world by distancing myself from it, focusing outwardly on the lives of others so that I could understand the habits of being, or, more simply, what makes us tick. This seemed like an honorable profession, and I quickly decided that teaching others to write was for me. I felt that I could help launch others into an orbit around their lives so they too could look back at the world in wonder.

I was excited by the prospect of my students' lives becoming poignant and compelling stories. I wanted them to realize that their stories made a difference: they can win for you the love of those who don't love you; thaw relations between you and others; take an axe to the frozen sea inside.

But my students, who were mostly male, rarely shared my tastes. The majority favored Bret Easton Ellis and Chuck Palahniuk, writers who specialize in the kind of violence and obscenity found on cable, albeit with—it would seem—tongues firmly planted in cheek. At first, I thought I could deal with the difference in taste—at least they weren't dull writers. (In Ellis's *American Psycho,* a vain corporate psychopath in an Armani suit and Hermès shoes kills hookers for fun. In Palahniuk's *Fight Club*, young corporate zombies take back dignity lost as office toadies by beating the tar out of each other in dank basements and plotting a series of vigilante attacks that will bring about the demise of consumer mall culture and a return to a *Leviathan*-like existence of hunting and gathering.) Admittedly, I encouraged my students to explore these themes: the undoing of the American male; testosterone run amok; Nick Carraways of the world unite and take up arms against your aggressors! But after

two years of homages to these writers—even though I believe imitation to be one of the best ways to teach writing—it became
clear to me that my students didn't hear the irony in Ellis's and
Palahniuk's voices. I seriously questioned whether the popularity of
these writers was due to what they saw as prophetic depictions of how
American culture creates moral monsters, or how capitalist culture
perverts American decency. There was no substance. No second
layer. For the most part, their stories read like bad movie scripts:
scant exposition; clichéd dialogue; coincidence-driven plots; beautiful, shapely and easy women; improbable sex and violence.

When Chuck Palahniuk gave a reading at the University of Pittsburgh, the line of students was literally out the door—I'd never
seen such a turnout for a writer. But the packed Q&A session was
moderated not by a professor of literature or even by one of the accomplished novelists from Pitt's creative writing program, but by a
screenwriter and filmmaker. Most of the questions had to do with
the film adaptation of the book and the process of how a book becomes a movie.

I couldn't help but feel that everyone in attendance was missing
what Palahniuk was really saying. He told how he wrote *Fight Club*
in his spare time while working as a mechanic. He spoke of his love
of writing and telling stories, of the vast research he does in prepa-
ration for each book. He talked of being inspired by Edgar Allen
Poe, of wanting to write modern stories of horror (albeit stories in
which a young man's intestines are ripped from his anus by the
suction of a pool drain while he attempts to masturbate). But the
aspiring male writers in attendance were not inspired by
Palahniuk's dedication to his writing; they were dazzled by his fame,
the possibility of the movie deal, recognition on the street (a phenomenon Palahniuk was getting used to). For them, this was not

about being a writer; this was about making money, being famous, being remembered.

Here was a more serious and complex problem than I had ever imagined. I was encouraged that so many young men were showing up to learn the craft of fiction, a craft that involves empathy and imagination, qualities not much valued in men these days. And to be fair, some were. But the majority of them seemed hemmed in by two ideas of being a young man in America. There was the gangsta rap, backward baseball cap, frat party and humongous football stadiums way of life that, looking out at my classroom everyday, I can honestly say they were ensconced within, and then there was the more urbane, "literary" affluence of East Coast, Ivy-League-graduate culture that they read about—designer drugs, drunken beach bonfires out of some Abercrombie and Fitch ad, ski trips, European jags in search of "oneself."

As I sat in the audience listening to Palahniuk reluctantly answer questions as to whether any of what he wrote was based on his own experience, suddenly it made utter sense to me: Brett Easton Ellis and Chuck Palahniuk (the authors and their characters) reflected this frustrating struggle back to them in the form of young men who are materially successful, well-fed and good-looking, but emotionally bereft.

I saw that the world of contemporary publishing wasn't (as I long believed) the world according to Nick Carraway—quiet introspection and unassuming observation—but Andy Warhol—a world where violent spectacle is a must, integrity is provincial, ideas are cheap (easily duplicated), friends are a means to an end and soullessness is de rigeur. My students believed Warhol's prediction: they were frantically reaching for their fifteen minutes. I was too, by thinking that *I* could save them.

WARHOL, AN ALOOF, HOMELY, EFFEMINATE, eastern-European Catholic kid from Pittsburgh, turned on his camera and recorded fame's sublimely ugly, and at times repulsive, wages. He filmed his "Superstars" shooting up and melting down. Warhol liked his actors compromised, malleable, pliant. According to Warhol biographer Wayne Koestenbaum, his approach to directing was much like "torturing performances out of his cast."

In *Vinyl*, Koestenbaum writes, a young man is subjected to aversion therapy:

> [Victor] is tied to a chair, a mask over his face; electrical tape binds his chest, hot wax drips onto his flesh, and he is force-fed "poppers." The inhalation is not simulated. Progressively more stoned during the movie, by its end he is incapacitated, and we feel we're watching a snuff film, a document of genuine torture.... Edie watches the torture of Gerard but she doesn't comment on it; at one moment in the film, she dances with him, but otherwise she remains in a separate, observing sphere. Perhaps she dances to distract herself from the nearby torture. Perhaps she dances to narrate it. Perhaps, for Edie, dancing is torture—her tormenter the offscreen director who licenses her perpetuum mobile.

I think of my wife taking her seat in the electric chair, or pulling the trigger on a revolver, hoping the flip of the switch or the explosion of the bullet would throw open the door to another world far beyond Slidell, Louisiana.

I think of Charles Graner directing Lynndie England to hold the dog leash, telling Sabrina Harmon to smile and strike a thumbs-up pose before the dead body of a detainee packed in ice.

. . . . .

I WRITE ALL THIS NOW AS THOUGH I KNEW IT in April of 2004 when the first photos of Abu Ghraib were made public. But I didn't. I hadn't gotten that far yet. I was still thinking of them as documents of abuse. I hadn't yet considered the photographer's intent—candid snapshots of life through the eyes of disgruntled, "weekend warrior" Army reservists. Disgruntled because of their unglamorous, thankless jobs watching over "low-value" detainees in what one of my college roommates, stationed at Abu Ghraib for the past several months, calls a "Hell hole." Their thrills came from posing and manipulating these human beings in positions that both attracted and repulsed them.

Nor had I thought yet about my own need for these painful photos. My need for an image of the war to latch on to, to help define it for me, to make an effigy of and rally around as arguments against the conflict. I sat with those photographs and, like many Americans, I fear, simply reveled in their horror. But then something happened. Weeks passed, and the feeling didn't go away. I was faced with the troubling question: Why?

Rereading Flannery O'Connor's "The Displaced Person," a story of a widowed farmer who takes in a family of Polish refugees fleeing the Holocaust, the images reached deep inside of me. Early in O'Connor's story, Mrs. Shortley, the snipey country wife of the farm's handyman, watches with suspicion and wonder as the displaced persons arrive. Upon seeing them,

> ... Mrs. Shortley recalled a newsreel she had seen once of a small room piled high with bodies of dead naked people all in a heap, their arms and legs tangled together, a head thrust in here, a head there, a foot, a knee, a part that should have been covered up sticking out, a hand raised clutching nothing. Before you could realize that it was real and take into your head, the picture changed and a hollow-sounding

voice was saying "Time marches on!" This was the kind of thing that
was happening every day in Europe where they had not advanced as
in this country, and watching from her vantage point, Mrs. Shortley
had the sudden intuition that the Gobblehooks, like rats with Typhoid
fleas, could have carried all those murderous ways over the water with
them directly to this place. If they had come from where that kind
of thing was done to them, who was to say that they were not the
kind that would also do it to others?

Reading this passage, I thought of the Abu Ghraib photos and
how they seemed to connect me to some point beyond the war, to
a fundamental truth about humankind—that within all of us is the
capacity for both great humanity and great inhumanity. Do Mrs.
Shortley's thoughts help us, the savvy modern viewer, to understand how images of death and destruction are interpreted from so
many miles away? On the one hand, they can be evidence of the
great barbarity of war, and on the other, they can be viewed dispas-
sionately as events that could only happen in such an unenlight-
ened part of the world.

The images from Abu Ghraib have been treated not as evidence
of acts of sin and barbarity against other human beings but as pure
deviance with no human origins except psychosis—a disordered
brain. America's response to atrocity on the part of its citizens has
been to deny that those particular soldiers "speak for us" or "represent" the larger good America stands for. This is the most harmful
response imaginable from a spiritual standpoint, revealing a profound misunderstanding of sin and evil.

In America, as in most cultures, evil, when found thriving in one's
midst, is "an embarrassment, a thing that one should diplomatically
distance themselves from," according to Reverend James Schall,
S.J.—an instinctive reaction that has serious problems. To step back,

to wash one's hands of evil, is to "make possible precisely the op-posite state to that which [the innocent bystander] desire[s]. For they actually multiply evil by leaving the field free to those who have little scruple with the good." Therefore, man cannot simply "with-draw" from the evil world in some simple or naïve fashion. For if one does not admit the possibility of the presence of God and evil in the same universe—which is logically what someone who wants nothing to do with evil really believes—only two alternatives re-main. Either God does not exist or evil is something that can be re-moved by unaided human effort.

In general, Americans have been convinced that diplomacy and reconciliation are tactics of the weak, not the brave and the free—an outright denial of the grace the Christian God extends to those who admit their sins and repent. Most Americans consider America a Christian nation in its promotion of life and liberty. But exactly whose lives and whose liberty is abundantly clear: Ours, not Theirs. By what distorted theology does this make America Christian?

As a kid, I always believed that Christianity and politics were sep-arate and surely not equal. Issues of faith were never ever discussed, it being such a *private* subject. Faith had no bearing whatsoever on current events, unless it was to pity those who suffered far away, or even right under our noses. Any twinge of guilt or feeling of re-sponsibility could be quickly snuffed out by the words of Jesus in Matthew 26:11: "The poor you will always have with you..." com-bined with a Puritanical belief that people must endure what is nat-urally, Providentially, theirs to endure. And they must do so with a smile and enormous gratitude for even being alive, and especially for being American. I came to believe that God had made some people poor and others rich, some handsome and others ugly for no other reason than to prove that He was in charge, when in fact, this is a heresy, a warped theological view that would by extension hold that $2+2=4$ because God made it so. Grace has been shamed and muscled out of Christian faith in America in favor of a Manichean worldview that sees cultural orthodoxy aligned with Good and cultural grotesqueness aligned with Evil.

This cultural grotesqueness—outright disagreement with the President, distrust of the government, criticism of the war in Iraq—is seen by American patriots as a fantasy view of the world based on the manipulation of facts by special interest groups and the liberal media. But for me, a Catholic, my sense of the grotesqueness of the world 2005 begins with Flannery O'Connor's stance that few people are able to recognize the grotesque when they see it, so cowed are they by advertising, polls, statistics and media reports that tell us the enemy is lurking "out there," not here under our very noses.

"We see what we want to see," a student recently said to me. I would add, "We see what it is easiest to see." What's both easy and difficult about Abu Ghraib is its familiarity, in that it reminds us so much of pornography, more so than the conscience-shocking photos of the Holocaust or Vietnam, Hiroshima or Matthew Brady's vast landscapes of Union and Confederate dead. There seems to be no outrage because these are not easily grasped photos of war—ignoble death and destruction—rather, these are photos that show people operating in that DMZ between pleasure and pain. Our culture's fascination and willingness to indulge—to revel—in the ambiguity of such images (Is it a head or an arm? Human or animal? Terrorist or civilian?) strikes me as one of the factors that causes humans to remain silent even when the war effort injures and kills innocent civilians.

. . . . .

WARHOL TURNED SEVENTEEN THE DAY the Enola Gay dropped Little Boy on Hiroshima, an event that is sure to have impressed him, if only for the iconographic mushroom cloud the bomb produced. Having grown up in a "bone-poor immigrant family" in Pittsburgh, Warhol's art has been seen by some as "an American response to American deprivation." But as an adult, Warhol prefered A-lists "to the exclusion of the human catastrophes inflicted and suffered by the United States, the country he adored." During the late sixties, the most politically polarized period of Warhol's lifetime, he chose not to make any overt political statements, so as not to risk pigeonholing or cheapening himself, ruining the sublimely naïve image of Andy by "taking a stand." Kostenbaum writes, "[Warhol] liked zing, oomph, vim, pizzazz—any hook, whether ad or accident, that could rivet the eye by exciting or traumatizing it... scenes you couldn't ignore because they aroused unholy fascination... Warhol appreciated any immediately recognizable image, regardless of its value."

Given this, it becomes increasingly difficult to see Warhol's story as one of follow-your-dream, rags-to-riches, or the artist as visionary/prophet whose personal obsessions exposed America's obsession with catastrophe: Jackie O, Marilyn, Elvis, Mao, electric chairs, lynchings, riots and car crashes. Warhol was not a brave and courageous man but a depressed and morally dislocated artist with enough Catholic sensibility to see that America's greatest art is not its plumbing, as Marcel Duchamp famously said, but its spectacularly banal violence.

I had this realization looking at the 2000 exhibit *Without Sanctuary* at The Andy Warhol Museum, a private collection of lynching photographs made between the 1890s and 1930s in small town America. Some images were made into postcards and were sent to relatives in other states as souvenirs.

Sontag wrote of the photos: "More than a few show grinning spectators, good churchgoing citizens as most of them had to be, posing for a camera with the backdrop of a naked, charred, mutilated body hanging from a tree. The display of these photos makes us spectators, too."

These horrific images were flanked by Warhol's own silkscreens of lynchings. Standing in a gallery of the Warhol Museum, I was repulsed by the original photos but felt nothing for Warhol's. And it wasn't just me. All around me, school children who had been bussed in from the suburbs to take in the show glanced at Warhol's, then quickly at the originals, then back at Warhol's, and then moved on to the gift shop. Warhol's images are executed with no passion, which requires an understanding of the events depicted. To Warhol, they were graphic and arresting, but what of the deep truth they reveal about humankind? I wanted some assurance that the students understood these photos weren't simply "random"—as young people like to say—or "demented." If the photos weren't being seen as evidence of the human capacity for atrocity, then what the hell is the purpose of such an exhibit? I cringed at the idea that they would go back to their classrooms and spend the rest of the day saying isn't it awful what *those* people did to those other people.

But why had Warhol's silk screens left me cold? His images of lynchings, car wrecks and electric chairs might be ominous, but they derive their ominousness, as with the majority of his paintings and silkscreens, from their clear made-ness and intention. They are reproductions of a reproduction, like photos in a newspaper, they seem to say *this exists elsewhere*. And while this statement of fact may entice our desire for exotic images of death, they ultimately fail to have the immediacy and mystery of an original photo's intention and history—qualities that would inspire fear and urgency in viewers.

MY WIFE ONCE TOLD ME SHE WOULDN'T HAVE known that there was a larger world beyond Louisiana and the Gulf Coast, where her family went every summer to vacation on what she calls the White-Trash Riviera, if not for a boy with floppy hair, cosmopolitan tastes and avant-garde aspirations. Her attraction to him is forgivable. She says that she learned something from him—how to be other than she was, to feign sophistication, but more important, that she should *want* to be other than she was. Both lessons helped her get out of Louisiana, to be a writer, to be successful, to charm people, to make them love her.

When I saw my wife for the first time, she looked like a woman who knew what she wanted. She was sitting at a small table in a coffee shop in Pittsburgh. She was beautiful, impeccably dressed and being hit on by a Swedish philosophy student whom I loathed. Not my type. Out of my league, I thought. But then I noticed that she was reading John Hersey's *Hiroshima*. It's one of the books that changed my life, I told her weeks later when I finally got up the nerve to talk to her. I was so nervous I couldn't think of anything to say. So I asked if she was reading the new edition of Hersey's book, the one with the extra chapter detailing the lives of survivors twenty years later. She said yes. Good, that's the one I read too, I said.

Weeks later, when I finally saw her apartment, I noticed her Warhol fixation—fridge magnets, a book case filled with dozens of books on his life, original Warhol prints in glass frames above her couch—a gift from an ex-boyfriend—"The only nice thing he ever bought me."

We sat on her couch, eating ice cream and watching *The Exorcist* on TBS. We often speak of that day as the most perfect day ever spent in the company of another person. It was the director's cut of the film, the one where Max von Sydow, sitting on the stairs just outside Regan's room, says sagely to Father Karas, (the troubled young Jesuit who has more faith in modern psychology than God), "The demon wants us to despair." It is a line that, to me, justifies the intense violence, the obscene language, the, heavy-handed special effects. If one cannot move past this trauma, this abomination, and see, even in the pit of such obscenity, that Christ compels the human being to reject Satan, to purify oneself by giving all away and following Him, then the day will be lost, as well as those subsequent. This one line, missing from the original film, held within it a truth so startling that later that night we talked about going to Mass, together. Neither of us had been in a long time.

Warhol said, "I love American movies because they're not about anything." *The Exorcist* suffered at the hands of critics who accused it of this and worse. The venerable Pauline Kael believed that the film lacked dramatic stakes—it was too easy, not to mention improbable. But more craven was the obscenity of exploiting a young child for box-office sales. The film can be easily read that way. However, with this line about despair, we—the woman who is now my wife and I—realized that the film, not despite the horrific images of Linda Blair cursing and spitting and profaning but precisely because of those images, was, if not spiritual, at the very least the cinematic articulation of a much-debated theological aphorism: The devil's greatest accomplishment is convincing the world that he doesn't exist. It is a film that causes the twenty-first century viewer to consider what the world looks like when God does not exist. Regan's mother is beside herself, the doctors are puzzled; not until every possible avenue has been exhausted does a doctor in a white lab coat suggest an exorcism. What seemed to be a medical problem is a spiritual one.

The images of the little innocent girl writhing in pain, tormented by the devil, are not merely cheap, titillating confections of stage make-up and Campbell's pea soup; they too are truly grotesque images because they connect us with a point in the distance, "not visible to the naked eye." In this case, that point is in the unseen, the spiritual world, a world that the majority of Americans believe exists but are not willing to consider as the source of violence and atrocity. *The Exorcist* is "about" something. It's about a culture whose faith has been bred out of it—like chickens whose wings have been bred off, O'Connor famously said.

. . . . .

IN SEPTEMBER OF 2004, FOUR YEARS AFTER the lynching exhibit, the Warhol Museum opened an exhibition titled *Inconvenient Evidence: Iraqi Prisoner Photographs from Abu Ghraib.* The exhibit was drawing scathing criticism from veteran's groups and supporters of the Iraq war from around the Pittsburgh region. The Warhol Museum, part of the Carnegie Museum system founded by steel magnate Andrew Carnegie, was receiving hundreds of emails from museum patrons, donors and year-round-pass subscribers complaining that the exhibit was inappropriate.

I was invited to participate in a panel discussion about the photos. On the day of the discussion I arrived at the museum early to take in the exhibit, which I hadn't yet seen. What I found was not what I expected. The photos, low-resolution reproductions of the original digital photos not enlarged or framed, were tacked to a white wall in an upper-story gallery of the museum in the same room as several of Warhol's huge canvases covered in camouflage patterns—clearly an intentional juxtaposition. To the right of the photos, on a placard, a statement by museum director Tom Sokolowski introduced the exhibit and posited some thoughts on their importance as artifacts. On a podium in front of the placard, a small guest book gave patrons the opportunity to comment on the exhibit and read what others had to say. Most of the comments I read ranged from puzzlement ("Is this art?") to negative ("This is unpatriotic." "What about the beheadings?"). In front of the exhibit on a small table, a binder containing articles from theorists such as Arthur Danto and David Levi Strauss, among others, as well as political commentators, concerning the photos and their "meaning" lay open for consideration. There was even a chair for patrons to sit down and take their time reading the articles. No one was taking advantage of the offer, although a few people hastily flipped through the binder and then walked out of the gallery.

On my way back downstairs to meet my fellow panelists I bumped into a group of my students whom I had bribed with extra credit. They all looked nervous about being surrounded by Warhol's work. One female student said to me, looking around with wide eyes at the pen-and-ink drawings of nude men, "I thought Warhol was just soup cans and Marilyn Monroe."

Downstairs I met the panelists: Henry Krips, a professor of media studies; Adel Fergany, past-president and board member of the Islamic Center of Pittsburgh and professor of computer science at a nearby university; and Linda Benedict-Jones, photographer, director of the Silver Eye Center for Photography and former curator of the Polaroid Collection in Cambridge, Massachusetts. We shook hands, but we did not talk about what we were each going to say. We took our seats in the front row of the theater.

Linda was to begin the event with a brief slide presentation of "photographs that changed the world." Then poets from Cave Canem, an African-American poetry collective founded by poet Toi Derricotte, were to read poems inspired by the photos on exhibit. Then there was to be discussion.

I had my misgivings about the exhibit being held at the Warhol, which I kept to myself because I thought that a public discussion of the photos was remarkable in itself. Although I wanted very badly to point out that Warhol was a master manipulator, an exploitative, deeply disturbed man who was not in the least concerned with causes—he was not anti-war, nor was he concerned with the oppression of other peoples. He reveled in the images that sparked so many other artists to become politically vocal. Warhol's political cachet came posthumously at the hands of art theorists and influential collectors. Warhol wanted to be remembered, to be a big star, to come from nowhere and make himself known.

The Warhol Museum's press release described the exhibit this way:

> Transmitted over the internet, the digital photographs from Abu Ghraib prison made the public aware of shocking human rights abuses and jolted international and American perceptions of the Iraq War. They also signaled a sea change in the representation of war through image-making technology. In addition to traditional means of media coverage, society is now able to see the Iraq conflict through the eyes of the men and women who were empowered to fight it.
>
> "As an artist, Warhol challenged boundaries, took risks and maintained a vital link with the emerging present," says Thomas Sokolowski, director of The Warhol and co-curator of the exhibition. "As an institution in his spirit, we see it as our role to continue to challenge, take risks and explore the relevant issues and expressions of our time. It's The Warhol's mission to be a vital forum for dialogue around contemporary issues such as this."

These photos definitely would have interested him as "expressions" of the "emerging present." They are photos from the new war—the War on Terror—an endless war, which has required the removal, or at least slackening, of previous safeguards that served to protect the innocent, not to mention the dignity of human beings.

The photos are the missing link needed to finally indict and seriously question the defensibility of the morally-lazy notion that "war is hell." It no doubt is. But the photos do not speak of a "posthumous reality," as Sontag has said of incriminating images that come out years after the fact. These photos were so recent they were undeniable, breaking the seal of silence that has long surrounded allegations of abuse on the part of the military interrogators in the War on Terror, and setting the stage for frank discussions of what American citizens will allow to be done in their name.

On this count, Warhol's legacy pales in comparison to the work of artists such as Francis Bacon and Leon Golub, artists who openly grappled with the human capacity for brutality and disintegration; but, who, due to the grotesque images they imagined and their toxic demeanors, were seen alternately as pariahs and geniuses.

But the Warhol Museum got something very right in regards to Warhol's artistic sensibility and the Abu Ghraib photos: The photos would have aroused him.

The lights in the theater were turned off and the slide show began. Photographs, now huge, were projected ominously above our heads. Robert Capa's famous photo of a Spanish partisan being shot. The burnt and mutilated remains of a lynching victim hanging from a tree. Iwo Jima. The first photo of an atomic mushroom cloud. A photo of a shadow left by a woman on the concrete steps of a bank in Hiroshima when she was vaporized by the heat from the bomb blast. A photo of a sit-in protest at a Woolworth's lunch counter in Jackson, Mississippi: a young white man and woman sit in solidarity with a black woman; behind them a wall of angry white protesters scowl and pour food and drink on their heads. A terrified, naked Vietnamese girl runs away from her village, which has just been napalmed by American aircraft. South Vietnamese police-chief General Nguyen Ngoc Loan executes Viet Cong Captain Nguyen Van

Lem. Last came one of the Abu Ghraib images: the iconic hooded detainee standing atop a box with wires attached to his fingers. Seeing these images together in succession, accumulating one on top of the other, was overwhelming. When the lights came up I slowly made my way to the long table on stage. I sat down and stared at my scribbled notes, but none of them seemed to matter a damn. As it neared time for me to make my first remarks, I realized that I was trembling. It seemed to me that any commentary was futile. When it came my turn, I apologized in a shaky voice and then did my best to remember what I'd wanted to say, stopping every now and then to clear my voice which continued to shake and break.

In my head, I was seeing these images alongside the video of Rodney King. I was seeing video of "smart" bombs entering through the windows and chimneys of Iraqi military targets in Gulf War I. I saw piles of charred bodies, aftermath of the Dresden firebombing. I saw the rubble of Ground Zero. But the American public has chafed at such comparisons, and rightly so. Very few of these images capture what Abu Ghraib captures.

The Q&A focused on the lies of the current administration, the fictions fabricated to make war inevitable, the lack of concern for human rights, the harm the photos caused to Arab–American relations. But we never talked about the photos: what they showed and what they didn't—the audience members, mostly white liberals in their late 50s, were blind with rage over what they perceived to be the obviously jingoistic foreign policy of the Bush Administration.

After the panel, I walked off the stage into a crowd of eight or so of my students who were waiting either to congratulate me, or to make sure I noticed that they showed up. The first question I asked was, "What did you think of the slides?" I gestured to the screen behind me where the terrible images had been. They looked around at one another and shrugged their shoulders. "They weren't so bad," one said. "Yeah, I didn't think they were so awful."

I was floored. Already thinking of how I would write this moment, I asked point blank: "Do you think that violent images just don't have the same effect on your generation?" A leading question, I know, but I needed to hear someone actually say it. A voice from the back of the group said, "I've seen worse at the movies."

Certainly we have. *The Exorcist*, with its unspeakable images of an innocent child spewing forth the most vile language imaginable, ultimately delivers us to a point of despair, where modern medicine exhausts itself. The images of Abu Ghraib evoke a similar disbelief, a tendency to seek a modern answer instead of an ancient one. The modern answer is abnormal psychology; the ancient problem is the existence of evil.

We are reluctant to acknowledge that evil exists within our midsts. We are much more comfortable speaking of "problems" (as they are susceptible to solutions) and "bad apples," "isolated incidents" and "random" acts of violence; this language allows us to discreetly compartmentalize so as to "move on" and begin the "healing process."

But photographs of violence and destruction, as Sontag has written, haunt. They aggressively assert their hard facts: a naked Vietnamese girl burned by American-delivered napalm, a black motorist being beaten by white cops; a young woman smiling over a dead body. Sontag writes that images of war speak a "universal language of destruction," a language whose poignancy is due to the innate human desire for order and harmony, edifice and wholeness. Looking at a picture of a bombed building we secretly, unconsciously imagine it whole again.

America is often described as a Christian nation, perhaps because it understands and appreciates this "universal language of destruction." Our history begets our duty to help the oppressed.

More than any other people, we respond mightily to images of destruction; we are moved to action by any perceived "hatred of freedom." As such, America should be a place of overwhelming compassion for the poor, the oppressed and the war-torn.

Sadly, this is not the case. America considers itself Christian not because it understands a universal language of destruction, but because it speaks a language of easy redemption. Redemption is at the heart of Christianity—*Corinthians 6:20: For you are bought with a great price. Glorify and bear God in your body.* Christian Americans have historically seen this country as a land of redemption. Joseph Smith, the founder of the Mormon Church, is believed to have received a prophecy from God that America would be the seat of the New Jerusalem. The Puritans saw America as the "New Israel"—a place free of oppression, where liberty and self-government would reign. In the 1840s, this Puritan belief informed the Jacksonian ideology of "Manifest Destiny"—that America was divinely chosen to spread democratic freedom all the way to the west coast. Woodrow Wilson's anti-isolationist foreign policy, while not employing explicitly-religious rhetoric, positioned America as the champion of the oppressed, promoting the self-determination of ethnic peoples oppressed by colonial occupiers, a policy that would later inform U.S. military intervention in the politics of Latin America, Haiti and Cuba. The Christian message of redemption has been grafted onto the myth of America, so that gradually American political thought and rhetoric reflects a belief that American power can restore human dignity to the oppressed and resurrect order where before there was chaos.

Such an ideology isn't, in itself, heretical. And with the spilling of so much American blood on foreign soil in "redemptive" missions, we feel we have earned our role as selfless redeemer, a god-like entity that may occasionally commit atrocities but only in service of the greater good, God's will. As a result, Americans have tended to interpret the language of destruction seen in war photographs differently, much like O'Connor's Mrs. Shortley does, as reminders of the darkness and crudeness of other people in other lands.

The Abu Ghraib photos do not show torture or death or even physical harm. They show "fooling around," "letting off steam," "abuse" rather than "torture." They are merely "humiliating" the prisoners, nothing more. Yes, humiliation is precisely what is contained in these photos: the robbing of dignity, the exploitation of the body in order to arouse feelings of power. What else are we to do with images of humiliated and dead enemies? We do not strain to see them alive again, do we? The virtuous impulse to turn away from force, to eschew violence, is overpowered by our need for redemption.

Flannery O'Connor once received a letter from a reader who said that when she came home at the end of the day she wanted to sit down with a book that "uplifted" her and that her work was not filling this need. O'Connor replied simply that if the woman's heart was in the right place she would have been uplifted. The letter and O'Connor's response strike to the heart of America's zeal for redemption. O'Connor's work was accused by main-line Protestants and Catholics as needlessly violent and morbid. She was asked again and again why she insisted on depicting America as though it were a Godless and violent frontier. She replied in her essay "The Fiction Writer and His Country":

> In the introduction to the collection of his stories called *Rotting Hill*, Wyndham Lewis has written, "If I write about a hill that is rotting, it is because I despise rot." The general accusation passed against writers now is that they write about rot because they love it. Some do, and their works may betray them, but it is impossible not to

believe that some write about rot because they see it and recognize it for what it is.

... My own feeling is that writers who see by the light of their Christian faith will have in these times, the sharpest eyes for the grotesque, for the perverse, and for the acceptable. In some cases, these writers may be unconsciously infected with the Manichean spirit of the times and suffer the much discussed disjunction between sensibility and belief, but I think that more often the reason for this attention to the perverse is the difference between their beliefs and the beliefs of their audience. Redemption is meaningless unless there is cause for it in the actual life we live, and for the last few centuries there has been operating in our culture the secular belief that there is no such cause.

In short, while we cannot treat the Abu Ghraib photos as we would a short story, we can witness in their public reception an acute "disjunction between sensibility and belief," one that calls attention not to a difference but a similarity in belief between author and audience.

. . . . .

COMING FROM THE MIDWEST, I WAS the perfect audience for F. Scott Fitzgerald's grotesque and haunted vision of the East Coast, a place of immorality and shallow dreams. I was uplifted by the ash heaps and extra-marital affairs. I saw myself in Nick Carraway, a man who finally revealed Gatsby as a man who believed, to a fault, in the power to redeem oneself. But now I wonder. Is Nick Carraway really a man of principle, or is he a dupe, complicit in the whole mess by allowing himself to be so taken with Gatsby, so fascinated by the ugliness and vanity? If he is a dupe, then I am too.

At the end of the book, after Myrtle Wilson has been run over and Gatsby has been killed, Nick yearns for his days as a young man returning by train from school to his home in Minnesota:

> When we pulled out into the winter night and the real snow, our snow, began to stretch out beside us and twinkle against the windows, and the dim lights of small Wisconsin stations moved by, a sharp wild brace came suddenly into the air. We drew in deep breaths of it as we walked back from dinner through the cold vestibules, unutterably aware of our identity with this country for one strange hour before we melted indistinguishably into it again.

Whether I knew it or not, and I certainly doubt that I did, I was in love with this air of superiority that came from thinking that I, like Nick, knew myself and my country. That I could rest easy knowing that all was right with the world and that any evil that might creep in would, in the end, be rooted out and shown to contribute to the good. Knowing this, I felt that I too could be like Nick Carraway and go explore for a while in the dark, know that I could leave any time I wanted, just pretend that what I had seen and experienced had never happened, and go back home where all was good and true.

But pretending, buying into self-made myths, is the first step toward ruin.

All this time I've been trying to piece together my wife's previous life and how I used to think before I met her, so that I may be able to understand how we came to be together. I have been trying to imagine what she was thinking when she agreed to sit in that chair and wait for the warm sting of electricity. What did she think when her boyfriend produced that gun? I imagine for my wife there was a scary, breathless moment of indecision in which she asked, *What are you planning to do with that?* I can't help but wonder if she was more attracted to him in that moment when he showed her the gun, held it up in the light and explained how it worked, let her hold it while he stood behind her showing her how to spread her feet apart, hold it parallel to the ground, site it, how the safety worked— clickety-click—all as a way of making her calm, as a way of associating lethal protection with love. I need to slow these moments down and imagine her thoughts because they are moments arrived at by small concessions, seemingly insignificant agreements and polite decisions not to resist. Because it feels too good, or maybe just new.

The images from Abu Ghraib prison tell a similar story. To pose as Lynndie England, Charles Graner and Sabrina Harmon did with those detainees took a conscious decision not to offend, to keep up appearances, to play along in the name of loyalty and love.

VI

. . . .

Prime Directive

"Today we'll see just what kind
of monster I am."

. . . . . .

Army Spc. Charles Graner,
on his way into court

I'M STANDING UNDER A STREET LAMP at the end of my street dressed as Captain James T. Kirk of the Starship Enterprise, wearing an extremely tight red long-sleeved shirt, layered over a black t-shirt to imitate the black piping around the uniform's collar, black slacks and black leather shoes. I'm speaking via communicator—a brand new cell phone, the kind that flips open—to Mr. Sulu, who had agreed to pick me up at this intersection of streets. I ask for his ETA. "Five minutes, Captain," he says. I clap the cell phone shut, and it chimes cheerfully. I wait. I look up at the trees and the darkening sky. At that exact moment, the streetlight above me hums loudly and then goes dark. It is the Saturday night before Halloween; the world seems rife with omens.

I meant to go to evening Mass, anticipating the next morning's hangover, but I couldn't bring myself to walk the block to St. Bede's because the priest, a poor man's Max von Sydow, is cold and unceremonious, and I didn't want him ruining it for me. Now I'm regretting it. I could've used the reminder that we are on the eve of a holy day. And I could have used the blessing.

My wife has taken a job in another state, and I can't join her until the semester ends and I've turned in my grades. So I'm living in our almost empty apartment, sleeping on a camouflage army cot. The wood floors creak more loudly now that there is nothing to deaden the sound—no hall carpets or crammed book cases, no tables or chairs, no pictures on the walls, just a stack of six phone books that we found under the couch that I'm hoping to recycle and a closet full of lonely clothes hangers. I feel I'm beginning to understand the Japanese aesthetic. Everything sits on the floor—my computer, lamp in the shape of the Eiffel Tower—and it's all accessible from the sitting or kneeling position. It humbles me. The house seems smaller now, not bigger. I have so little that I am more aware of the mess I make. I don't like it. So I stay out of the house until late at night and I always drink a few beers to help me sleep.

I flip open the cell phone and scroll through my list of contacts; I need company. That's the genius of the thing—it cuts the loneliness. I wonder if there is a patron saint of space travelers.

Out of the darkness beyond the street lamp, a couple emerges arm-in-arm. They are middle-aged, wearing brightly colored expensive-looking hiking jackets. Like most residents of the neighborhood, they appear well fed and in shape; they have attractive haircuts that suit their facial type. I try to look inconspicuous. I run a hand through my over-gelled hair. I check my watch and look expectantly down the street. I flip open the cell phone; it makes a xylophonic noise; I arbitrarily push buttons to give the appearance that I have official business here. As they pass I nod and say "Hiya doin," very colloquial and provincial—friendly-seeming. It isn't so difficult to navigate this world if you know a few of these mannerisms and sayings, even dressed as I am.

A big red Chevy truck comes over the rise in the street. I step off the curb and wave.

Sulu reaches across the seat of the truck and opens up the door. He's grinning ear to ear, wearing a mustard yellow shirt, black slacks and shoes. We laugh at how authentic we look. I hand him his communicator, an old deactivated cell phone borrowed from a friend. He's beside himself with how perfect it is, how silvery and space age. He hands me a shiny silver chevron badge indicating that I am an officer of the Starship Federation. It, too, is perfect, almost an exact replica of the real thing I've see on television. I made it from a Pabst Blue Ribbon can, he says.

As Mr. Sulu and I drive, I think to myself: I shouldn't be going out. I should be grading papers or working on my novel, or reading one of the five books I hid from the movers. I should be in

Indiana helping my wife hang pictures, or raking leaves, (she tells me a wind storm came through and defoliated the huge oak) or standing on a chair installing the new dining room chandelier, or sneaking up behind her in the hallway and kissing her hair. Instead, earlier in the day, Mr. Sulu and I drove to Dick's Sporting Goods in the Waterfront Mall to buy long-sleeve shirts, on sale.

Our first stop is a pre-party at a shotgun flat in Friendship. In attendance: a Prozac pill, the Cracker Jack Kid in blue and white sailor suit carrying a stuffed dog, a soccer referee, a cowboy, and Miss Scarlet from Clue, the whodunit board game. Miss Scarlet is carrying a noose, but wishes it was a wrench instead; she's afraid that people will see her as just another beautiful suicide.

The rail-thin Indian kid hosting this little warm-up lap says to me, with an accent that modulates between British, Indian and golden-haired surfer from Santa Cruz, "You're one of the extras, right? One of the guys that dies when they beam down to a dangerous planet? They wore red shirts, didn't they?" Mr. Sulu corrects him, "He's Captain James T. Kirk!" I think about trying out Kirk's melodramatic delivery, *Spock, have you lost your Vulcan mind?* But I'm not feeling up to it. No one is drunk enough for it to be funny, including me.

All of us sit in the living room, drinking and smoking. We compliment one another on our costumes and tell stories about previous Halloweens, but most of the conversation is about *Star Trek*—favorite episodes, favorite characters, favorite spin-offs. The thing is, I'm not really a *Star Trek* fan. When the soccer referee, who happens to be a graduate student in Philosophy, mentions the Prime Directive, neither Sulu nor I know what he's talking about.

"No, really," he assures us, "it's very interesting." The Prime Directive is the moral code that governs the conduct of all Space

Federation members; it says no Star Fleet personnel may interfere with the healthy development of alien life and culture.

The room erupts—we've hit upon something. *Star Trek* is a morality tale! Someone rattles off the different ethnic backgrounds of the characters—It's like the United Nations! The Klingons are the Soviet Union! Someone else breaks in, "It's like trying to introduce democracy to Iraq!" Bush is a war criminal! Iraq is another Vietnam!

The election is only two days away—the most important election in a generation.

There's a feeling that the Prime Directive will help us to solve this crisis.

This is an informed group of people—would-be philosophers and writers and psychologists, a dynamite auto mechanic with a degree in geography (he can name nearly every world capital; he knows the location of each ocean and sea). I listen to the laundry list of confirmed atrocities: over one hundred thousand Iraqi civilian casualties, according to Britain's top medical journal; no weapons of mass destruction in sight; hundreds of detainees held without charge in Guantanamo Bay, Cuba.

But nobody mentions Abu Ghraib.

I decide it's best not to bring it up; it'll just bring everybody down.

Prozac begins to get impatient; she's ready to move on to a party at a friend of a friend's house in Shadyside—the official university psychology department party. We finish our drinks, smoke down the last of our cigarettes and file out the door, still buzzing about the possible connections between Iraq and the Prime Directive.

The party is lame. Only a handful of people are in costume, dressed as Pittsburgh Lolitas, dulled visions of the Oakland Catholic girls who wait for the bus outside the Carnegie Museum in short, pleated skirts and knee socks no matter the weather. I expected more dark ingenuity from psychology students.

In line at the keg, a guy in a big afro, bell-bottoms and polyester shirt open to reveal his thin chest hair says, "Beam me up Scotty." Noticing my red shirt, he points and laughs: "You're one of the dudes that dies, right?"

I push my way back through the house, past the table of people playing a drinking game, through the empty dining room where a klatch of Lolitas are grinding to Outkast, through the slender hallway where stoic, plain-clothes boyfriends wait in line for the bathroom, out to the front porch.

I'm alone now. All is surprisingly quiet except for the thump of bass through the windowpane behind me. I feel like maybe I'm sabotaging my own good time, so I think about trying out a Captain Kirk imitation. This requires a little method acting. I try to find my own points of emotional connection to Kirk's identity: There are long pauses in my own speech. I slow down at the ends of sentences to allow time to formulate the next thought (something a forensics teacher in high school told me to do to avoid saying "Ummm"). But what I can't tap into is Kirk's confidence, his bravado, his unfailing sense of duty to ship and crew. I'm a coward. Lately, I'm afraid to open my mail.

I know it's silly, but I think back to the Prime Directive and the war in Iraq. I think of my enlisted cousin who, at my grandmother's funeral, dressed in his Marine uniform, said that he couldn't wait to bomb Iraq into the fucking Stone Age. I think: in two days, George Bush will be reelected; the draft will be reinstated; my students, who have been reading Susan Sontag's *Regarding the Pain of Others* and Tim O'Brien's *The Things They Carried,* will be drafted and will experience first-hand what we have tried to understand from all angles all semester—what Sontag concludes we cannot ever understand, no matter the candidness and explicitness of the reportage, no matter how many reporters are imbedded, no matter how freely the images flow. War is indiscriminate. It lays waste to everything.

Miss Scarlet comes out onto the porch and sits down in the chair next to me. "Is anything wrong?" she asks. "No," I say, trying to shake it off and have a good time, "It's just that…" I pause. I look around for something else to blame. I nod toward the picture window behind us, "It's just this music." Outkast has given way to Chingy—*I like it when you do it right thurr, right thurr.* And even though it's petty, for that moment the music becomes a part of it too. I can see the video in my head: the big-butted girls in short shorts and skirts and shiny bikini tops in a subway car white-knuckling the silver poles, squatting low to the floor and somehow causing their rear ends to vibrate.

Everything is out of balance. I weigh the blurred faces and genitalia of Abu Ghraib detainees against the near-naked, big-breasted, big-assed women gyrating on the subway. I weigh Charles Graner's look-what-I-caught smile and the pyramids of human bodies against the costumed psychology PhDs grinding in the living room. In between songs, they stand in line at the keg discussing psychotic behavior and dementia.

Scarlet smokes her cigarette and tries to make conversation. She talks about how rap used to not objectify women. This makes me more depressed. She recognizes this and gets up and goes back to the party. Despite myself, I watch her walk away from me and see beneath her short skirt, fishnet stockings.

Suddenly, Sulu appears on the porch, followed by the entire cast of characters. "Let's go, Kirk," he says into the communicator in his palm.

We've heard that the next party has a roller coaster and a fun house, kegs of beer, hot dogs and hamburgers, all for ten dollars and all under a giant circus tent. Prozac tells us there may be a wait to get in; priority is given to people who bought tickets ahead of time. But I am determined to stay out, away from my empty house, away from thinking, so I climb into the back of Cowboy's Suburban. As we travel towards the party, someone passes around Iron City tall boys. I take one and almost immediately I am feeling it again, the Thing in me that is always restless. I crack open the can and a stone is rolled away; there it is, blinking its eyes.

The house is set back from the street behind a high hedge, its upper stories hidden by old trees. It looks plain haunted. Tiki torches frame the front steps and the costumed partygoers who sit there, smoking. Behind them, the arms of the wide, dark porch open to greet us. But the front walk lists off to the left through a break in the hedge, and we follow the gathering noise around the side of the house. Here, the tree limbs sag low, so we have to duck. When I stand upright again I am at the end of a line of costumed people, all of them turning to look at me with frustrated eyes.

At the front of the line there is a gate, and on the other side, one hand resting on it, is a man in a tailored ivory suit. I immediately dislike him. His neat haircut, Roman nose, that snake-oil twitch to his mouth and left eye. The way he stands there at the gate, all smug and proprietary, from time to time glancing back over his shoulder and assessing, judging from the noise, a party in full swing.

A group of Catholic School Girls brushes past me; they smell like perfume and cigarettes. "We have tickets," they chirp. "We have tickets." The man in the ivory suit inspects their tickets, opens the gate and points toward a table behind him. After they pass, he shuts the gate and walks behind a hedge, out of sight.

Violent scenarios flash through my head, things reasonable people would never do. I imagine leaping the fence and tackling the man in the ivory suit and grinding his face in the lawn. I envision the orgiastic, Hieronymus Bosch-like party beyond: stilt-legged half-man half-birds wearing strange pointy caps and copulating with young maidens before the yawning maw of hell, demons playing never-before-seen musical instruments. But I blink the images away. I think about going home. I think: *This is ridiculous. Why am I waiting in line?* But thinking this, the vision returns—the orgy, the maidens, the fire, the roller coaster, the fun house. I need some proximity to strangeness, something to take my mind off of the stuff that was waiting for me when I was alone.

When the man in the ivory suit finally lets us in, I am in no mood to make conversation with anyone. I look for the food. There is none left. I look for the roller coaster. It is closed. The fun house? No one knows what I am talking about. Cowboy gives me a beer from his shoulder-carry cooler and I stand motionless in the middle of the crowd, watching the people go by, making a list of the predictable costumes: vampire, zombie, fairy, flapper.

Then I see him. I think we had a class together once. But he looks different. He's grown a mustache. He wears pale green rubber gloves, an olive-drab t-shirt, army-issue pants and black combat boots. He is wearing glasses.

Slowly, I recognized his costume. I feel my face animate. I step around a group of people and thrust my hand forward and shake his rubber-gloved hand. I smile and shake my head and say, "Look at you." I just can't stop smiling and shaking his hand, like we haven't seen each other since childhood. He smiles back, a little bashfully, as though both happy and annoyed at being recognized, like a celebrity in the airport.

He hands me a few Polaroids, and I look closely, having to squint in the dim light of the tent. I hold them up toward the little light there is. They are pictures of people with their faces covered, and my friend is kneeling next to them, smiling into the camera, giving a thumbs up. I must have given him a puzzling look because he produced a Polaroid camera and a black sack—"a sandbag," he says.

It takes a moment for it to come together, for the two to add up to what I've seen on television and online and in the newspapers and magazines. It is like he's made an improvised bomb from household cleaning products—it isn't so much that it is wrong, it is that he thought to do it. He has actually gone through with it, gone beyond the point where rational people turn back, chicken out, shake their heads and laugh it off.

It is somehow exhilarating.

"Do you want a photo?" he asks. "I thought we would take a photo together, just the two of us"—Captain James T. Kirk, the fearless leader of the Enterprise, with army specialist Charles Graner of Uniontown, PA. He turns away from me and scans the mob of people under the tent. His eyes fix on the back of a tall kid talking with a circle of women just a few feet away. He taps him on the shoulder. "Excuse me, would you mind wearing this?" He shows him the bag. He points at the camera and makes the international symbol for "take a picture," the index finger moving up and down in a motion like depressing the button. The tall kid shrugs and smiles as he puts the bag over his head. Graner's girlfriend steps a few feet away to properly frame us up. It is only then that I notice she is in costume too—army-issue shirt, pants and boots. My old buddy, Graner, kneels down on one side of the kid and I get down on one knee on the other. I give the thumbs up. I smile.

—FLASH—

Splotches of color dance before my eyes. The mechanical whirring as the grey tongue of film shoots forth from the camera. Dazed by the flash, I thank the tall kid and shake his hand. "No problem."

Now it's awkward between us. There's not much else to say. I tell Graner it was good to see him, he says the same, but before he walks off with his girlfriend into the crowd, he hands me the Polaroid. I put it in my pocket before anyone sees.

Not sure what to do now, I stand on the sidewalk in front of the house and look for a ride home. A group of partygoers is huddled there waiting for cabs. An actor kid I know is there with his arm around a girl dressed as a cat. I can tell he doesn't remember my name. "Hey," he says and smiles. "You're one of those guys that dies, right?"

The next morning in the shower, I replay the previous night. It takes some time to remember how I got home. Cowboy's Suburban, I think. I vaguely remember laying back in one of the beanbag chairs that serves as his back seat, watching the houses pass. I work backward from there, trying to piece together the night. That's when I remember the photo. I panic. I turn off the water and hurry out, hair dripping, to search the pockets of my pants. There I am, kneeling and smiling and giving the thumbs up.

I call my wife in Indiana. I feel like I have to tell someone. But when I tell her about the Graner costume, she is horrified. "That's so sick." I decide not to tell her about the picture. I'm too ashamed. I put it in a shoebox in the empty closet and try to forget about it. But I can't. I lie back down in the army cot and analyze what I've done from every conceivable angle.

I want to be upset, but I can't make myself see that kid dressed as Graner as the sick, disrespectful one. What's wrong with me? I think about the meticulousness of the costume—the exact color of rubber gloves, the mustache, the Army issue clothing, the glasses—and the picture taking. It was his way of showing that what went on in Abu Ghraib was not a case of "a few bad apples," but a case of what we've all become, what we're all capable of.

But no one at the party batted an eye. No one else seemed to notice him. He was ignored. Was I the only person who recognized him?

Then it got scarier. I thought, wait, there's another wrinkle. Not only was he was acting it out, and calling me to act, but he documented it, gave me a memento that proves I was there: and not only did I do nothing to stop it, I participated in it.

The still images we'd all seen on the news, on the internet, had become useless, inert, lifeless—they required work on our part, work to imagine the suffering of others, work to insert ourselves into their large, unspeakable silence. As a result, the Abu Ghraib photos are inconclusive. They became no more than a handful of soldiers playing at the boundaries of torture.

But then it's so easy to moralize the situation, become polemical about it. Those soldiers were hicks from the sticks; something in their environment made them this way. In those photos, they were acting out their sick fantasies of power on the poor detainees.

Have we come to expect nothing more from people like Graner and England, who we imagine to be from tacky trailer parks in dead-end hollers? Don't we rest assured that these are the kinds of people who join the army because they are easily manipulated by promises of cars, money for college, patriotism and simply getting the hell out of Nowheresville, USA?

Educated, metropolitan people could never do such things; we are too aware, too aware of the ways in which we must respect one another's differences, too aware that any amount of cruelty is uncivilized and culturally reprehensible. These kids from the sticks make perfect soldiers because they naturally hate what is foreign.

It's a tragic plot in that it is inevitable: The hero can do nothing other than what he was born (and raised) to do. But we have to remember—as I am forced to remember when I think, shamefully, of posing for that photograph—our capacity not only to hate, but also to sympathize with the tragic hero. This is the part of tragedy that exposes our own violent, desirous, prideful human natures, and also our capacity for true sympathy.

Inevitably, we meet ourselves coming and going.

I posed with Graner, and by doing so, humiliated those victims all over again. But didn't I also commemorate them and mourn them? This was more than just post-modern satire. In that moment, Graner and his prisoner were alive, in front of me.

I recall being eighteen, in college at Notre Dame, and watching a group of students pass the steps of my dorm following a lone man shouldering a large wooden cross. I remember how disgusted I was, but how later I wished I had stopped what I was doing and followed.

This practice of recreating Christ's Passion is not a metaphor. You actually participate in the condemning of the Lord, and by doing so, become mindful of the fact that man's sin made his death inevitable. It's this mindfulness that makes the difference.

If I am not mindful of what I've done, I'm nothing but a ham, a pornographer. If I am mindful, the photo might become sacra-mental—a reminder of my fall from grace.

When we deny that we have anything in common with Graner and the others who are pictured in the photos, we allow all that is most despicable and ugly in our nature to thrive. If we are too proud to see ourselves in those photos, to realize that, as Sontag wrote in the *New York Times*, the photos are us, then we have no hope of finding any meaning whatsoever in them. They will simply haunt us, without any understanding of why.

Halloween is when unsettled souls roam the earth. Under that circus tent, past midnight, we were all roaming, asking to be seen, looking for connection. I found it.

. . . . . .

ON HALLOWEEN NIGHT, MY ACROSS-THE-STREET neighbor, Mel, the revolutionary, a man who claims to have run guns for the Black Panthers back in the day—his minivan plastered with bumper stickers proselytizing, "Religion is the what keeps the poor from murdering the rich," and, "George Bush: International Terrorist" and "Universal Health Care NOT War"—came over and asked if I'd help pass out candy to the trick-or-treaters. Mel is a kind, loving man, even if we don't see eye to eye on religion, so I agreed. This is something my wife loves doing; it would remind me of her. A pathetic act of atonement for what I'd done the night before.

At dusk, I crossed the street to Mel's. I found him in the dining room, rooting through a box of Halloween masks. He told me to pick one out. He held up a gruesome yellow-fanged beast with squinty dread-filled eyes. He looked me up and down and told me that I needed to wear something with long sleeves—"So they can't see your skin. And something to cover your neck, like a hood."

He showed me a black dickey that he wore to cover the skin the mask didn't. I did what he said and came back up the front steps just as the first trick-or-treaters were coming up Mel's walk.

Out of the corner of my eye, I watched as this indisputably good man, whose first thought in the morning is "How can I help others today?" laid down next to the table where the bowl of candy sat and went limp as a scarecrow. When the two kids, both maybe ten years old, reached the top of the steps, I said hello and pointed, "The candy's on the table." They walked to the table and as the first dipped his hand into the bowl, Mel sat straight up and roared, "WHAT'RE YOU DOING?" The two kids screamed and ran from the porch. Mel stood up and with his mask still on, laughed and laughed.

The man was giddy—I mean scarily pleased with his ability to cause small children to hyperventilate. I watched him do it again and again. One young mother yelled "Hell, no!" and bolted down the front steps, leaving her wailing children frozen with fear to the porch boards.

Finally, after an hour of watching, Mel, asks me, "Why don't you try it?" So I do. I put on a mask with a bony grim reaper-like visage and lay down on the porch and become very still, like a dead man. I can hear the little ghouls coming. I hear their feet on the sidewalk and then on the steps. My heart beats harder. I try to slow my breathing so that they won't see my chest rising and falling, but it does no good. I try holding my breath, but this just makes me panic. The footfalls pause inches from me. Then I hear them talking to one another.

"Is that a real person?"

I can smell my own breath; my breathing is loud.

"Kick him and find out."

VII

. . . .

City of Lost Souls

IT'S A CASE OF HER WHITE WORD AGAINST his black one, and it takes little deliberation among the angry patrons of a barbershop on a sweltering night in Mississippi, at the height of a drought—"sixty-two days without rain"—for the men to form a posse to track down Will Mayes, a black man rumored to have raped an unmarried white woman, Miss Minnie Cooper. Without a thought to his potential innocence, the men jump into two cars and zoom off into the pitch-black night down the dusty roads toward the ice plant where Will works. When they find him they usher him into a car and then drive farther out into the rural dark of Mississippi, finally turning on to a road leading to some old brick kilns that are said to be bottomless. Will Mayes, needless to say, is never seen again.

I tried teaching this story once to a college creative-writing class in Pittsburgh. It's by William Faulkner, I told them. It's titled "Dry September," and it's a story dealing with racism and violence. For some reason, I felt that I needed to warn them. I was worried that they would be upset by the darkness and violence of the story. Faulkner's narration is third person, describing the sweaty, mad, lustful search for Will Mayes with a distance that doesn't allow you to get close enough to know the thoughts and motives of these men, making them simply brutal creatures known only by their quiet, hissing voices and their resolve to make sure someone pays for what's happened to Minnie. When they come upon Will at the ice plant, they don't ask him if he's guilty; they simply tell him to shut up and push him into the waiting car. We never know his exact fate. We are only told by one of the nameless members of the lynch mob that we won't be seeing him anymore. Meanwhile, it becomes clear that Will's victim, Minnie Cooper, has lied about the incident in order to gain the attention of the men of the town, who prior to this saw her as a cold, asexual spinster. Now heads turn as she walks down the main street.

I think it's one of the most haunting stories ever written by anyone anywhere. To me it is a perfect, almost holy, story. Perhaps it reads a little like a parable in its distance from the events, its stepladder view of things, a slight angle and elevation that raises the events to the level of mystery. But to the reader who knows anything of the 1930s South, what has happened to Will Mayes is no mystery. So I was surprised and even depressed to find that my students found it dull, cliché even. Haven't we heard this story enough? said one student. Another said, it was too much of the same old theme—yeah, we know that people used to be violent bigots. The largest group of students felt that Faulkner had shirked his responsibility as a writer—taken the easy way out—by not spelling out Will Mayes's fate to us, as though Faulkner had robbed them of full disclosure and thus closure of the matter, to be shut of it, to have solved the crime.

It rattled me to think that this story was deficient in any way. I had to catch my breath for a moment and rethink my whole lesson plan. I was blown away because it was all so clear to me. The story speaks to deep truths of race and gender, obviously, but more importantly, it dramatizes what it would be like to live in a world where people just disappear without a trace, where people are just plucked from their daily lives—poof!—erased. I put it to my students this way: What if you lived in a world where this happened on a regular basis; your friends one by one go missing without a trace. No eyewitnesses. No leads. Moreover, you suspect that many people must know what has happened to your friend, but no one will help, they are too afraid to speak out. By the time I had finished my rant it was the end of class. The board was filled with inscrutable scribbles that no one but me could understand. The poignant reality of the story had taken me over. I was stuck inside it, unable to communicate what I felt was its clear brilliance.

Reflecting back on this day, now five years past, I've had time to rethink what went wrong. And it seems that the story, because of its "modern" style and the distance of the narration—which doesn't foreground the individual perpetrators, but rather the blind hatred of the lynch mob—deprives modern readers of a satisfyingly simple villain, a scapegoat on which to focus our disgust, thus leading my students to dismiss "Dry September" as poorly-executed art. "Is there even a plot?" I remember someone asking. From this perspective I can see that the story must have seemed like one relentless hot gush of prose.

I also think we are generally afraid of confronting such a huge dilemma as racially-motivated violence. What can I do in this situation? How can I alone confront racism? These feelings of futility are common, so common that they frustrate us, so that we are upset that we even have to deal with it. It becomes easier to just not deal with the situation, especially when put to us in such an oddly distant way.

In order to understand my love of the story I have to go back to when I first read it. It was a warm day in September of 1996. The class sat in a circle around the professor in the grass of South Quad, fifty yards from statues of the evangelists Matthew and Luke, which stand sentry on either side of another sculpture of Jesus and the Samaritan woman at the well—the parable in which Jesus reveals that he knows the woman's entire history: She has had five husbands, and the man she lives with now is not her husband. This display of psychic power has always scared me; it comes off as showy, but it also seems to be just the right use of power. It causes this woman to consider that this man is the Christ.

Of course, none of this was on my mind at the time. I was more fixated on the evil of racism, reveling in the absolute ugliness of these men, and self-righteously identifying with the Barber, the one man who tries but fails to reason with the men that they must find out the facts before condemning Will Mayes. Today's media would probably hail him as "courageous" for trying to stand up to the leader of the lynch mob, McLendon, who, Faulkner tells us, commanded troops in the Great War and was commended for his valor. The Barber's no pacifist, but he wants prudence. He follows McLendon and the others, hoping to talk some sense into them. He knows Will Mayes and Minnie Cooper and it just doesn't add up. There's something off about the situation. By today's standards he is not what you can call a hero; ultimately he fails. In fact, while the men are struggling to push Mayes into the car the Barber is accidently struck in the face. He retaliates by punching Will Mayes. We are left with no clear hero, just the sinister promise by another veteran of the War, younger than McLendon, "We're just going to talk to him a little; that's all."

"We're just going to talk to him..." It's the most often used euphemism for violence that I know. The oddness of the phrase isn't so much that it's a lie used to placate those against violence, but that it shows outright scorn for dialogue, as well as a lack of trust in the rule of law. The euphemism renames the violent act so it can be spoken casually and without guilt. An everyday example would be rhinoplasty, more euphemistically, nose job, more euphemistically "work," as in, "I'm having work done." All of these definitions stand in for the violence and invasiveness of the literal procedure: I'm going to cut open your face and peel back the skin and then take a grating device, much like a cheese grater, and grate down the bone. The surgical euphemism distracts attention away from what we call the side effects, the aftermath. You will have some bruising, swelling and bleeding. In other words, you'll look like you've gone twelve rounds.

Later in Faulkner's story, after Will Mayes has, we assume, been lynched, we overhear two men discussing his fate. "What did they do with the nigger? Did they—?" "Sure. He's all right." "All right, is he?" "Sure, he went on a little trip."

Consider the euphemisms that have been bandied about amidst the on-going investigations into widespread allegations of torture and abuse of detainees in American military prisons: "Letting off steam," "sport," "hazing," "working out frustrations." Then there are the slightly more official terms used by the MPs guilty of abuse at Abu Ghraib: "soften up" and "make sure he has a bad night." And then there are the most official, legal terms which come to us from the Department of Defense and the Pentagon: "set conditions for interrogation," "stress positions," "environmental manipulation," "water boarding."

In college, euphemisms dominated our speech and our pitiful knowledge of sex. We didn't speak in as careful and calculated a language as Defense Department lawyers, we spoke more like, and probably fancied ourselves more on par with, elite groups like the Navy SEALS or Green Berets, communicating in head nods, hand signals, shifting eyes and acronyms. Lunch conversations, conversations during crowded dorm-room parties, conversations in the basement study-lounge of our dorm, were dominated by comparing lists of sexual euphemisms and other apocryphal stories of drunkenness and stupidity. Acts that would make our mothers faint, but, to be sure, things that no one had actually done. At the time, the fun of hearing about these colorful descriptions was that there was always at least one person in the room who didn't know what a Savannah Sling or a Rusty Trombone was. The group of us would say, "You don't know?! Oh man, wait till you hear this." And then there would be the long debate about who would tell it. "You tell it. No, you. I can't, man, it's too gross." Even-tually, someone would get up the courage, pretending not to care, shaming everyone else for being a bunch of Nancys. We just all wanted someone to say it. It was so salacious and disgusting as to not be believed. And we would watch the person's face who didn't know what was coming so we could see their reaction, which ranged from the deadpan—that's demented—to the hysterical, where the kid would get up out of his chair and run out of the room and down the hall, just for effect. It's no fun when no one laughs, because then it becomes clear that we're just a group of sad, hormone-addled college dudes with no girl-friends sitting in a study room on a Thursday night.

It's the euphemistic description of violence, or descriptions of violence through a kind of shorthand, that is most directly at the heart of my first experiences with violence—on film. I loved the way movie stars seemed to always find the cleverest, most memorable ways of speaking even under great emotional and physical duress: "Hasta la vista, baby." "Say hello to my little friend." "I made him an offer he couldn't refuse." In fact, for most of my life I have idolized those who can come up with witty, memorable one-liners on the spot, having many times been in situations where I realized halfway down the stairs what I should've said. Speaking in euphemisms makes us seem quick, clever, decent; it disguises our essentially brutal nature.

This same phenomenon exists in the world of torture. The use of euphemisms here is common, creating, according to Ervin Staub, a "shared group culture and less[ening] the torturer's confrontation with the meaning of his or her actions."

> The electric chair is known in some South American countries as the "Dragon Chair."

> In Greece and other places, torturers referred to each other as "Doctor."

> "The Bar," "The Chicken," and "The Parrot's Perch" are all synonyms for "tying the wrists together around the bent knees and

then pushing a pole behind the knees. Suspended like this, apart from suffering extreme pain the victim may have the blood and nerve supply cut off and, of course, it leaves the victim vulnerable to beating all over the body...."

"The House of Fun" officially known as "prisoner disorientation equipment": "a high-tech room fitted with a generator for white noise and strobe lights such as might be seen at a disco, but turned up to a volume capable of reducing the victim to submission within a half hour."

"The Telephone": Blows to the ears and the side of the head resulting in burst eardrums, permanent hearing loss, deafness and blindness.

"The Submarine" or "Waterboarding": Dunking the victim in a tub of water in order to "simulate" drowning. Can lead to permanent lung damage.

I was exposed to the idea of euphemisms watching *A Clockwork Orange* in Joe's basement. Little Alex and his droogs speak of their brutal conquests in their own violent adolescent slanguage, Nadsat. Stanley Kubrick's film adaptation of Anthony Burgess's book was released in 1971, and it was a controversial box-office success. As in the book, the vulgarity of Alex and his gang's actions is masked by silly, yet sinister, banter.

As Burgess's book illustrates, torture and abuse are most often committed by groups, as it is in groups that individuality is lost to a collective identity. In the military, this collective identity is necessary in bonding soldiers together in a common cause, while also creating a meritocracy in which following orders is motivated by the promise of moving up in rank. But it goes deeper than just following orders. According to psychologist Ervin Staub, the real issue at stake in a situation like Abu Ghraib, where military policemen and women say that they were ordered to "rough up" detainees, is that when groups are thrown into distressing situations like the over-crowded, under-staffed prison, the "perception of reality will be shaped by [the group's] shared belief system." In the unconventional War on Terror, it seems that these shared beliefs have to change in response to the beliefs of the enemy, instead of remaining steady according to military code or international law. In other words, the group has the power to define the "correct" or morally acceptable reality, "making deviation from the group unlikely."

Stanford Professor Philip Zimbardo's famous 1971 prison experiment, in which college students were arrested, booked, strip-searched, deloused and incarcerated in a mock-prison guarded by their peers, saw much of the same behavior reported by detainees and seen in photographs from Abu Ghraib—verbal abuse, denial of clothing, and pornographic abuse were all observed when they believed that no one was looking. Reflecting on the experiment, which was cut short due to increasing abuse, Zimbardo surmised that in groups, the "normal" college students lost "their personal identity and experience[d] deindividuation, with a lessening of the power of social prohibitions." In other words, those acts which the students may have seen as objectionable and even unconscionable before entering the group were allowed, for fear of "endangering one's status in the group."

But unlike Zimbardo's experiment, where the students assumed roles in a familiar system of justice defined by guard and prisoner, Abu Ghraib, Bagram and Guantanamo were and are places where the boundaries of justice and accountability are foggy, given the Presidential order to treat prisoners humanely, even if they aren't protected by the Geneva Convention. As we have learned through interviews with soldiers—like Captain Ian Fishback of the 80th

Airborne division, who said that abuse of detainees at forward operating base Mercury was allowed as long as no one "came up dead"—in environments such as these, guards begin to feel outside the rule of law, a belief that promotes a culture of abuse and wanton disregard for an already hated enemy.

While this explanation may seem facile and broad, implicating a range of groups from the Shriners to the Boy Scouts, we must focus on how such a description helps us understand the lack of protest in the case of those soldiers who came into contact with Charles Graner.

News reports tell us that Lynndie England's defense team used expert testimony from a school psychologist who has known England all her life to claim that she had a "very complex language-processing dysfunction," causing her to be "overly compliant in social settings, especially in the presence of perceived authority. . . She would seek some form of authority in order to follow. She almost automatically, reflexively complies." I'm not sure what a "language-processing dysfunction" is, but it sounds similar to what I'm trying to describe here: that the moral reality of the actions photographed and video-taped at Abu Ghraib are shaped in large part by the language learned to describe the actions that went on there.

Consider reports of prisoner abuse and murder at the hands of American soldiers at Bagram Airbase in Afghanistan—the second front in the War on Terror, therefore not receiving anywhere close to the same attention as Abu Ghraib, despite the fact that two plainly innocent men are dead, beaten to death by American interrogators. The abuses that lead to the deaths happened over the course of two weeks in December, 2002 (more than a year before the now infamous incidents at Abu Ghraib) but were only brought to light in an article by Tim Golden in the May 20, 2005 edition of the *New York Times*. This article might not have been written if Staff Sergeant W. Christopher Yonushonis, an interrogator stationed at

Bagram, had not come forward and asked to be interviewed in August of 2004. What was to be a quiet internal investigation turned scandal. Yonushonis's testimony brought to light a fact that, according to Golden, had been overlooked in the investigative file: "Most of us were convinced that the detainee was innocent."

The detainee is only known as Mr. Dilawar. According to Golden and Army reports, Mr. Dilawar was a twenty-two-year-old taxi driver who was detained along with his three passengers in connection with a rocket attack on an American base. During the course of interrogation, Mr. Dilawar, "a frail man, standing only 5 feet, 9 inches and weighing 122 pounds," was struck about the legs more than one hundred times in a twenty-four-hour period, to the point where, according to the autopsy report, the detainee (referred to at Bagram as a P.U.C. or "Person Under Control") died from heart failure due to "blunt force trauma to the lower extremities," essentially a blood clot. At a pre-trial hearing for one of the accused soldiers, the coroner, Lt. Col. Elizabeth Rouse, testified that Mr. Dilawar's legs "had basically been pulpified." She further added, "I've seen similar injuries in an individual run over by a bus."

The tactic that left Mr. Dilawar and another Afghani man dead was known among the MPs at Bagram as the official sounding "peroneal strike," a blow to the side of the knee, not part of military training, that was imported by soldiers with prior experience as guards at correctional facilities in the U.S. This "strike" is known to incapacitate the receiver, but if used too often, it causes permanent knee injury. The deceased received countless such "strikes" for reportedly shouting for "God's help" and for acting "haughty."

In defense of what happened at Bagram, Staff Sgt. Steven W. Loring, the noncommissioned officer in charge of the interrogators, told investigators, "There was nothing that prepared us for running an interrogation operation."

At the time of the abuse, ten months had passed since President Bush gave the executive order that the Geneva Convention did not apply to Al Qaeda or members of the Taliban because neither were signatories to Geneva. Bush may have insisted that detainees were being treated humanely, but Utah reservist Sgt. James Leahy told Army investigators that the order was interpreted as giving interrogators license to "deviate slightly from the rules.... There was the Geneva Convention for enemy prisoners of war, but nothing for terrorists."

Sgt. Leahy told investigators that legal and historically effective forms of interrogation, such as trying to establish a rapport with the detained, were discouraged: "We sometimes developed a rapport with detainees, and Sergeant Loring would sit us down and remind us that these were evil people and talk about 9/11 and they weren't our friends and could not be trusted." Loring's actions illustrate what Zimbardo found in his experiment: "It is probably impossible to act [violently] toward other human beings without progressive devaluation of them, without a spread of disregard for their welfare and their humanity."

The three passengers in Mr. Dilawar's taxi that day were eventually sent to the Guantanamo Bay prison and held for a year before being released without charge. Later they would receive letters in the mail notifying them that they posed "no threat" to the American military.

What could fuel a group of soldiers to continue to beat a man after it was clear that he posed no threat and that most believed to be patently innocent? What should be our, the American public's— an overwhelmingly Christian public—reaction to acts of violence against innocent people caught in the wide net the United States and its allies have cast? To think about this we have to think more practically from the point of view that we inhabit most of the time: the watcher.

First and most importantly, the viewer of the news does not have to meditate long upon the actions of the American soldiers at Bagram because only a small amount of time is devoted to reporting it on the evening newscast. We become susceptible to what Neil Postman has famously dubbed the "Now...This" format of television news. Due to a limited amount of "available time" in a news broadcast, each news item is afforded only a brief window of exposure, usually forty-five seconds, a window rarely commensurate with the magnitude of the event. Given that there are no photos to support these reports from Bagram, sadly, the story fails to meet one of the most, if not the most, important criterion for newsworthiness—an image.

The second reason why Bagram did not cause significant moral outrage is that it was already "old." The incidents at Bagram took place nearly two years prior to Abu Ghraib, thus violating the other essential criterion for newsworthiness: that it be new. Bagram, in the wake of Abu Ghraib, although it happened first, was no longer current. Its moment to be relevant had passed. In effect, any major news coverage given to Bagram ran the risk of being seen as "digging up the past."

But the most salient reason why Bagram, Abu Ghraib and Guantanamo have not caused a significant political backlash in the United States—again, the nation with the most people claiming to be Christian in the entire world, nearly 225-million people—is that many Americans see the deaths as just unfortunate, merely "collateral damage."

There are many complex ways of explaining this fact. The first possibility is to focus on the American republic's shift from a view of virtue as stemming from biblical teaching—Mosaic Law (the Ten

Commandments later fortified by Jesus' Sermon on the Mount)—to favoring state and national law in which morality is not an operative term. So rather than consider the morality of an act, we focus on the legality of an act. The second is that given the religious plurality of the United States, where several dozen denominations of Christianity exist side by side, not to mention hundreds, if not thousands, of non-denominational churches with memberships anywhere from twenty to twenty-thousand, no one can agree on just what kind of life Jesus intended his followers to live. The question of how to balance faithful Christian practice and American citizenship proves rather difficult.

Nations cannot be Christian, only individuals. And while it may be true that all those who believe in Christ are united in one body, they quickly find themselves at odds with one another, divided by those things that belong to Caesar.

Bill McKibben, a life-long Methodist, points out in his scathing *Harper's* essay "The Christian Paradox: How a faithful nation gets Jesus wrong":

> Only 40 percent of Americans can name more than four of the Ten Commandments, and a scant half can cite any of the four authors of the Gospels. Twelve percent believe Joan of Arc was Noah's wife.... Three quarters of Americans believe the Bible teaches, "God helps those that help themselves." That is, three out of four Americans believe that this über-American idea, a notion at the core of our current individualist politics and culture, which was in fact uttered by Ben Franklin, actually appears in Holy Scripture.

This could be the most damning statistic of all. How else could a nation that so strongly self-identifies as Christian—President Bush has said that Jesus Christ is his favorite philosopher—stand silent in the face of such barbarity?

We were supposed to found a nation under God that would be an acropolis beyond reproach, a beacon of light shining in the moral darkness of the larger world. How has it fallen to us, the United States, to be so despised?

By helping ourselves. Our mandate from God helped us to assume the role of moral superpower, a nation dedicated to defending freedom and the oppressed. But the vast majority of attention given to the issue of torture has not focused on measures to ensure that human beings are not tortured, but in legalistic squabbles over what constitutes torture and what is merely the necessary force to extract intelligence that may head off future attacks and bring terrorists to justice. American might is being applied in an end-justifies-the-means manner, with no thought to either the human rights of those innocent people who happen to get in the way or the moral imperilment of our soldiers.

The American military insists that anyone caught abusing power is a bad apple, but what happens when the entire structure of the war effort is built around sacrificing a few bad apples to save the bunch? We are taking liberties with human rights with the understanding that individual soldiers on the ground make easy scapegoats.

The term scapegoat comes from an ancient Israelite ritual in which a goat bearing the sins of Israel was driven out into the wilderness. According to Rene Girard, "The high priest placed his hands on the head of the goat, and this act was supposed to transfer onto the animal everything likely to poison relations between members of the community. The effectiveness of the idea is that the sins were expelled with the goat and then the community was rid of them." The feeling of reconciliation provided by scapegoating was so powerful that it became addictive, to the extent that the Israelite people "attempted to reproduce the ritual [on their own, but] without shame."

The desire to achieve redemption without repentance echoes Flannery O'Connor's judgment of what she saw as the modern attitude toward "redemption": Everyone wants it, but no one stops to consider its real cost. O'Connor believed that Christianity's scapegoat, Jesus, changed the essential nature of scapegoating. By accepting the sin of mankind into himself, Jesus, through his death and resurrection, destroyed sin and death—sin no longer controlled man. The stakes of redemption are, as a result, very costly—no less than the death of the wholly innocent, Jesus.

This is not an arcane or controversial theology. This is the core of Christian belief. So those Christians who believe that the Abu Ghraib photos show nothing more than a few demented soldiers reveal a great tolerance for violence and a belief that psychology has the power to redeem. We can diagnose and heal ourselves.

In this way, the Abu Ghraib photos are the very picture of the American soul in conflict with itself. Because even though "bad apples" have been punished and discharged from the military, and I imagine more court martials are to come, there still exists the *political* will of the American people to fight the War on Terrorism. The court martials suggest that the acts of Graner and England and others are isolated, not in any way a product of the way war is waged, thus exculpating American policy. The United States has the political will to keep fighting the War on Terror because we fear another September 11th, a true tragedy in every sense of the word, a graphic, dramatic event whose rationale is unfathomable, nearly demonic, and whose image of the Twin Towers collapsing is lasting and haunting—an event that should cause reflection on mankind, but has drawn more reflection on what it means to be an American.

. . . .

I'M SIX MONTHS SHY OF TURNING THIRTY, and I realize that I've forgotten all the dirty jokes I used to know. The high threshold I used to have for bawdy humor has been slowly, incrementally eroded by sobering accounts of rape, murder, brutality and torture found in newspapers, magazines and novels, and images of such acts in television and film.

The talk we talked in the dorm study lounge—these were things that would only be done with someone who liked it or deserved it because they were already bad, damaged, dirty, slutty. When we talked like this the women had no names or faces; they definitely weren't like anyone we knew, but girls we maybe would like to run into someday in an odd turn of events where we knew we would never see her again. We told stories—urban legends, really—of flight cancellations leading to overnight stays in strange cities like Cincinnati, Kansas City and Detroit. A woman from our flight asks to share a cab to the hotel. You have drinks at the bar, one thing leads to another, and.... This is when these things happen, far away from home, where no one knows our names, what we're like normally. It's like a stopover in a strange invisible city: a place that disappears as soon as you leave, a city that appears only at night, in bad weather, when you are filled with doubt, a city of lost souls searching for connection.

Sgt. Javal Davis, who served four months in military prison, the lightest sentence handed down, for his role in the Abu Ghraib scandal, called Abu Ghraib just that, "a city of lost souls," a place that would turn any soldier bad, "from *Gomer Pyle* to *Full Metal Jacket*."

To the soldiers stationed in these prisons—some of them secret "black sites" run by young lawyers who rule on who should be released and who should be detained, in addition to ruling on whether certain interrogation tactics are permissible within the scope of the current U.S. definition of torture—these are places where all the detainees are evil America-haters who withhold terrible secrets. They are inhospitable cities where the guard is just as much a prisoner as those in chains. Where the guards sleep is identical to where they sleep. What the guards eat is only slightly better than what they eat. The guards are outnumbered. Mortar and rocket-propelled attacks are nearly an every day experience, not to mention the serious over-crowding brought about by the constant influx of suspected insurgents—none of this was planned for. During a sandstorm they could break free and overtake the prison.

Why then should we be surprised that a group of newly recruited twenty-year olds with no formal training as interrogators repeatedly beat two chained detainees to the point of death, neither of whom had been proven of committing any crime.

This is Faulkner's Mississippi, circa 1930. And it is also Miss Eudora Welty's Mississippi, at the beginning of the civil rights movement.

Welty's brief but incendiary 1963 short story "Where is the Voice Coming From?"—loosely based on the assassination of NAACP organizer Medgar Evers—is told in the first person by a white man who has made up his mind to murder a young black civil rights leader. The story is one of the most startling depictions of the roots of racism ever written by a white writer. The narrator lies in wait for the young man at his home, and as he is walking to his front door, he shoots him. Standing over the body the narrator says: "There was only one way left, for me to be ahead of you and stay ahead of you, by Dad, and I just taken it. Now I'm alive and you ain't. We ain't never now going to be equals and you know why? One of us is dead." Later, he dispenses this advice to the reader: "Everybody: It don't get you nowhere to take nothing from nobody unless you make sure it's for keeps, for good and all, for ever and amen."

The images from Abu Ghraib suggest by their very composition— the sexual poses; the collegiate cheerleading pyramid of human

bodies; the cowering of prisoners before attack dogs; a smiling female soldier giving a thumbs up next to a dead detainee wrapped
in plastic, stuffed in a body bag filled with ice; a hooded detainee
standing atop a box, arms held out in a cruciform pose—photog-
raphers who needed to prove who was superior, once and for all.

VOL. CLIV .. No. 53,255

INTERROGATORS CITE DOCTORS' AID AT GUANTÁNAMO

ETHICS QUESTIONS RAISED

Pentagon Says Personnel Are Advisers Who Do Not Treat Patients

By NEIL A. LEWIS

WASHINGTON, June 23 — Military doctors at Guantánamo Bay, Cuba, have aided interrogators in conducting and refining coercive interrogations of detainees, including providing advice on how to increase stress levels and exploit fears, according to new, detailed accounts given by former interrogators.

The accounts, in interviews with The New York Times, come as mental health professionals are debating whether psychiatrists and psychologists at the prison camp have violated professional ethics codes. The Pentagon and mental health professionals have been examining the ethical issues involved.

The former interrogators said the military doctors' role was to advise them and their fellow interrogators on ways of increasing psychological duress on detainees, sometimes by

BOMBS PUMMEL CENTRA

An Iraqi came to the aid of a man whose clothes were on fire yesterday after
The attacks and several similar ones raised the death toll in the city to 43 si

VIII

· · · · · · · ·

Weavings of War
(Erie, Pennsylvania,
June 24, 2005)

FRONT PAGE OF THIS MORNING'S *NEW YORK TIMES* is a photo with this caption:

> BOMBS PUMMEL CENTRAL BAGHDAD An Iraqi came to the aid of a man whose clothes were on fire yesterday after four car bombs exploded in central Baghdad, killing at least 17 people. The attacks and several similar ones that began Wednesday raised the death toll in the city to 43.

The image is so horrible that I'd rather not describe it—I will, but not just yet. Instead, I'll tell you that I see this photo while sitting at a café table under a canvas umbrella at a Starbucks in downtown Erie, Pennsylvania. To my left I can see the colonnade of the Erie Museum of Art, across the street is the State News & Variety Store, next to that is the Richford Arms, a ten-story apartment building with a green awning. The Arms borders Central Park, where a Civil War memorial, a ghostly oxidized Union soldier, stands wearily against a backdrop of huge oak trees, and further back, fully beneath the shade of the oaks, is a public fountain where children splash and squeal. On a bench just at the edge of the park, about fifty yards from my table, a black man in silver reflective glasses lays his trumpet across his lap and clips a single sheet of music to a wire stand in front of him. He rolls his shoulders, puts the horn to his lips and begins playing taps. It's a warm breezy day, not a cloud in the pale blue sky. I look back down at the newspaper in front of me and begin writing. So far, it's been a strange morning.

This is where I've spent six weeks of every summer for the past four years, teaching creative writing to exceptional high-school students, kids whose talent is at times both life affirming and scary when I begin to think what I was doing at sixteen. It's the most rewarding job I've ever had. I look forward to it, especially after teaching four sections of Freshman Comp each semester for the previous eight months. It's a small bubble of creativity, a fairy tale land, like the enchanted island of *The Tempest*—nonexistent for the other forty-six weeks of the year—an invisible city of youth and beauty.

But much has changed since I took the job. Less than a month after my first summer on faculty, the attacks of September 11th occurred. Less than a month after my hope in fiction as an art form was restored through the scary talent of my students, I was feeling, as I watched the footage of jumbo jets slamming into the Twin Towers of the World Trade Center, that fiction was dead.

But I got over it. I met the woman who would become my wife; I started writing the novel I'd been putting off; I got engaged. Four months before the wedding I won a fellowship to an arts colony in the foothills of Virginia. There, I saw my faith in fiction renewed. I wrote for six hours every day, and at night I would play heated games of ping-pong in the basement of the residential quarters, drink Tennessee whiskey, smoke hand-rolled cigarettes under the gazebo while someone strummed a guitar. Some nights I would just gaze up at the millions upon millions of stars while floating on a raft in the colony pool. The sight of that many stars used to worry me, but in the aftermath of 9/11, when the unfathomable suddenly became fathomable, fiction reality, and with my wedding now only a few months away, I was able to push aside the terrifying emptiness of space and concentrate on the possibilities of my new life. But who was I kidding? The moment that I was alone, my thoughts would drift to the Abu Ghraib prison photos. One afternoon, just after lunch, I came into the TV lounge to see footage of an American pleading for his life before being beheaded. I couldn't write the rest of the day. I lay on the small bed in my studio and doubted I would ever finish the book.

That doubt only intensified upon leaving Virginia and arriving in Erie where my students, getting their first taste of colony life, were incredulous about the news out of Iraq. By the end of the summer I had scrapped the novel.

A year has passed since then. The war rages on. I'm married, and my wife is seventeen-weeks pregnant. This time next year my wife and newborn will accompany me, and this kind of early morning peace and quiet will be a thing of the past. And so it seems necessary to try to capture my thoughts at this moment, with so many things about to pass away and so many new things about to be born.

As I left my campus apartment for Starbucks this morning in Erie, I passed a small glass bus shelter that sits across the street from the Veterans Affairs hospital. I've driven past this hospital and looked up at its Spirit of '76 logo—one-story tall, red-white-and-blue striped "V" and "A"—many times, but this is the first time I noticed anyone waiting for a bus. There were two men in army-issue jackets, one stood and looked expectantly down the street, smoking. The other sat in a wheelchair with a large American flag attached to the back, like a cape.

Now, drinking my coffee, basking in the sun, my sunglasses on, I'm trying to think of constructive criticism for a short story we'll be workshopping later in the afternoon, but I can't concentrate. I'm distracted by the people passing by. I love to people watch— you never know when the face of inspiration is going to glide by. Staring at the street and buildings and people, I start to notice them—just a few at first but before I know it, seven, eight, nine, ten—men similar to those at the bus stop, short and tall, black and white, some in their camouflage uniform jackets with their last names stitched to their chests, another with a POW-MIA bumper sticker on the wheezing black motor box of his motorized wheel chair. These are not kindly elderly men of the Second World War with inky jailhouse tattoos of mermaids and anchors, or a heart with "Mom" inscribed across it on their forearms, wearing golf shirts and khakis just out for a walk, these are men in their early fifties— Vietnam vets—who look unhappy, some even devastated, all of them still wearing a part of their uniform.

I feel the various threads of a story coming together in my head, so I take out a legal pad and record what I see: An obviously meth-addicted man with red lesions on his face and calves limping down the street; two muscle heads in tank tops standing in the doorway of a storefront bodybuilding gym breathing heavily, walking off the adrenaline rush from a set of squats; two men on a tandem bicycle dressed in identical Hawaiian shirts and khaki shorts and floppy-brimmed Easter-Sunday hats. They wave at me and smile insanely as they pedal by. (After this, I see them nearly every morning here at the coffee shop, holding hands and working crosswords together, once working on their Spanish pronunciation of often used verbs from a book called *101 Spanish Verbs*.)

I finish my coffee and stop in at the Erie Museum of Art to talk with someone about giving my students a tour, perhaps leading them in some writing exercises responding to the current exhibit. Last year, when I stopped in there were maybe fifty pieces of art, mostly the work of local folk artists, spread out over three small rooms and a basement gallery. None of it caught my attention so I left. I was the only one in the museum.

When I walk in today the placard at the entrance to the museum stops me in my tracks. "Weavings of War" it reads, in a white, sten-ciled font—to look more military, I guess. The museum has just opened, and the woman sitting behind the desk looks surprised to see me. As I pay the admission fee—something like three dollars— she tells me about the exhibit. It features hand-woven quilts, tapes-tries, clothing and rugs depicting the violence witnessed by women from war-torn countries—places like Vietnam, Cambodia, Peru, Chile, Afghanistan and Pakistan.

From the admission counter I can see the first tapestry framed near the entrance to the gallery. Small, doll-like Vietnamese soldiers fire dashes from toy machine guns into the air at a squadron of American jet fighters, which fire cartoonish missiles that float in the space between heaven and earth. As I move closer, into the gallery, I can see that the soldiers and planes and wayward bombs are stitched into the fabric, a process that causes the panoramic battle scene to appear like the crude drawings I made as kid, when G.I. Joe was the rage and Cobra was the international terrorist organization of concern.

On the adjacent wall, two large tapestries detail Hmong refugees being slaughtered by Vietnamese soldiers as they flee their homes. In the next room I find huge story cloths by South African folk artists detailing police brutality, kidnappings and subsequent riots sparked by apartheid. In a short hallway connecting the two back galleries I find a small rug by an Afghani weaver crudely depicting the World Trade Center attack of September 11th—two airplanes coming from opposite directions, frozen in time at the moment of impact, like catastrophic mirror images; the noses of the planes are buried halfway inside the glass towers. But that's not all. In the middle of the rug the weaver has stitched the American flag next to the flag of Afghanistan, as if to show that our fates are united. In the last gallery I find still more rugs depicting the Twin Towers. One larger than the previous bears the words, "The Terrors Were in America." The largest rug in the exhibition is spread out on a raised platform in the middle of the gallery. This one is by a Pakistani weaver, one of the first rugs to emerge since the United States began its attacks to root out the Taliban in Afghanistan. The carpet bears a huge dove. Its wings are outstretched, and it seems to peer down on a low flying F-16 jet fighter and a Blackhawk helicopter, as well as a black tank.

When I return to the main gallery I feel that I have lost time. The cloths on the walls become more and more menacing each time I approach them. I see things I didn't before: small pools of blood represented by knots of scarlet thread and meticulously observed details on the sides of aircraft and tanks, detail that tells of the weavers' first-hand knowledge of these weapons. I'm dazed—caught off guard by the sorrow hand-stitched into the faces of protestors fleeing the South African police.

I go out to the main entrance and ask the woman if I can speak with the curator of the exhibit. She makes a phone call. While I'm waiting I find some even smaller tapestries I had overlooked be-fore—*arpilleras*. A card attached to the wall tells me: "pictorial ap-pliqués." They're the size of hot pads and they depict, again, with child-like simplicity, Chilean men, women and children being kid-napped by paramilitary forces. One depicts a 1979 protest where the Chilean Mothers of the Disappeared chained themselves to the National Congress building in Santiago and staged a hunger strike to call attention to the fact that their relatives were still missing. Another depicts the abduction of a woman's son by masked men. A mess of black yarn is stitched over her son's face to indicate that he has been hooded. I notice this same gesture in many of the small arpilleras—the black yarn symbolizing the blotting out of their very existence—disappearing them.

By the time the curator arrives my head is again filled by images of the hooded detainees at Abu Ghraib.

I introduce myself and tell her that I teach fiction writing, and that somehow I think this exhibit will be a useful, eye-opening ex-perience for my students. They have spent the last two weeks in front of flat-screen computer monitors typing at the speed of light.

I want them to see how other cultures record the stories that have shaped their lives. She likes the idea, and walks me through the gallery to point out some of the highlights.

She turns and directs my attention to a tapestry that I must have walked right past as I came in. It appears to be a simple ceremonial tapestry of African origin, no guns or tanks or bloody bodies, just a rectangular length of cloth with bands of rich naturally dyed pigments—pumpkin, leaf green and ochre—separated by intricate crosshatched patterns. The tapestry doesn't seem to be about war at all; more like something you'd see at the Natural History museum, innocent and folksy in contrast to the bombs and guns of the others. I mention this to her. "But look," she says, and walks to the wall and points to a pattern near the bottom of the five-foot long cloth, "Helicopters."

By God, they are, but only crudely, like the helicopters of the early Atari video game *Combat*, one dimensional, unable to show their destructive three dimensionality, their high-powered machine guns and rockets.

Next the curator points to a deep wine-colored Oriental rug hanging on the wall near the entrance. The border is intricately patterned. Inside the border is a background pattern of odd shapes, what appear to be exotic jungle birds—parrots maybe? In the center of the rug is another strange shape I can't make sense of at all.

But then slowly I begin to see, the beautifully patterned border is made up of a column of tanks, and the objects in the background that I believed were colorful birds are actually helicopters, and the huge odd shape that dominates the center of the rug is suddenly, almost magically, an AK-47 assault rifle with a banana clip.

The repetition of these weapons in a pattern made them melt into the background. Perhaps their very ubiquity on television as of late made them invisible to my American eyes.

I wonder how my students would respond to this kind of art, art that comes out of an oral culture. I talk with the curator as we turn in a circle, taking in all the panoramic landscapes of combat at once. We discuss ideas for presenting the work to my students. She pauses. She says she hasn't done anything like this before, but she reassures me that this is what the exhibit is actually about, oral cultures colliding with technologically advanced weapons of war. It's about overcoming the silence atrocity induces through story telling—memorializing pain and loss.

Two weeks later, when I take my students to the museum, I think about how to explain why we are going to see this exhibit, how it will benefit young fiction writers and poets. I think about telling them this long strange story of going out to get a cup of coffee and falling down a rabbit hole. I think about sharing what I wrote in my notebook that morning as I sat outside Starbucks, but I don't. It is nearing the end of the program, and they have all worked very hard for the past five weeks writing and revising, falling in love, having epiphanies, minor breakdowns and major breakthroughs. It seems cruel to subject them to the breakthrough I think I've had—it would be too hard to put it to them in a way that wouldn't seem trite or self-righteous, so I keep my mouth shut and let them just walk through the exhibit.

Although I want to quote to them Elaine Scarry: "Pain occurring in other people's bodies flickers before the mind then disappears."

I want to tell my students that the images woven into the rugs and quilts and story cloths depend on their stillness, their poverty of "realism," to speak truth to the powerful impressions left on the living, the memories emblazoned on the screens of their forever altered imaginations.

I want to repeat to them the line from Steve Orlen's poem: "The imagination is a terrible gift, cultivate it accurately."

I want to tell them: This is not to say that digital images, which can be effortlessly duplicated, disseminated quickly, narrated by commentators while being replayed at slow speeds on endless loops, from different angles, show us nothing of the truth. It just means that they show us something we are unwilling and unable to see— our complicity.

I want to tell them: This is why the crucifixion interested the atheist painter Francis Bacon. It was "an elevated example of man's brutishness," an example of what mankind does to its own while other people look on, unable and unwilling to know the pain being endured.

Pain, as Scarry writes, destroys the world, cuts us off, isolates us, makes us forsake what is most sacred to us. The end of Orwell's *1984* causes us to confront the choice we would make: "Put the rats on her! Put the rats on her!"

But I don't say any of this. I bite my tongue and watch as they politely wander around the gallery, some longer than others, and then leave for the Starbucks across the street, where they order Frappuccinos and sit in a big group laughing and loving life.

. . . .

I ENVIED THEIR BLINDNESS. I didn't know how else I could explain what I was seeing now all around me short of putting their fingers in the wounds of the dying, taking them on a tour of the VA hospital, walking them down to the park to sit and talk with the men who smoked and watched the children play.

No one wants to be the messenger. The messenger is threatened with death, accused of being insane. The only messengers that can withstand the assault are those true prophets who survive in the wilderness off locusts, who blind themselves with lye, and put rocks in their shoes and walk around town in the hopes that the pain will relieve them of the awful knowledge and visions. The prophet fumes, vents, stomps and assaults because at all times, the end is close at hand.

I'm no prophet. But what if the prophets didn't paint for us these grotesque visions of the world. What would the world look like?

Would we believe ourselves to be incorruptible, that justice is ever on our side?

What would the world look like? It would be a world of Here and There. Us and Them. Those who appear, and those who disappear.

T.S. Eliot said, "Humankind cannot bear very much reality." Donald Rumsfeld said, "Those pictures never should have gotten out." Out of sight, out of mind.

I want to believe that sooner or later brutality catches up with all of us, even if it is only through images on the front page of the newspaper, and it burns us clean, cuts us to the quick, causes us to see with new eyes. Which is where I found myself the morning of June 24, 2005 in Erie, Pennsylvania—looking with new eyes.

I was reminded that art—good art, that is, art that causes in us mysterious exhilaration—doesn't give us some silly, arbitrary, alternate world. It is not a lie fabricated out of whole cloth to trick you or do you harm or even titillate you. It is a promise that what you know to be true and beautiful will be challenged and sometimes affirmed, in a form that you could have never imagined.

What do the Abu Ghraib snapshots make us confront? God? Yes, but the god of war—Moloch, the savage, monolithic god of Ginsberg's *Howl*.

> *Moloch! Solitude! Filth! Ugliness! Ashcans and unob-*
> *tainable dollars! Children screaming under the*
> *stairways! Boys sobbing in armies! Old men*
> *weeping in the parks!*

Moloch, a "sphinx of cement and aluminum," who consumes brains and captures imaginations. It is he who tells us that our knowledge is superior and therefore so is our power. It is he who tells us our power is just.

Susan Sontag writes: "To photograph is to appropriate the thing photographed. It means putting oneself into a certain relation to the world that feels like knowledge—and, therefore, like power." We see ourselves seeing and believe that we are in control.

The photos of Abu Ghraib are an opening, an invitation to see pain and suffering as not pain and suffering. We begin to see as the photographer sees. We consecrate and consume the brutality. We eat evil bread.

This is what feeds the restive Thing inside us all—the Thing that rolls the stone away, opens its eyes, blinks. The Thing that divides us.

Here's what I wrote in my journal when I saw the photo on the front page of the *New York Times* on June 24, 2005:

> A man lies in the street, dazed. His body is totally blackened from the fireball that ignited his clothing and burned them from his body. (I'm reminded of the Vietnamese monk who immolated himself in front of the American embassy is Hanoi. Immolation: To consume oneself. To be consumed.) Only a small area on his shin is red and raw; the rest of him is black. A man stands over him, helping it seems, pouring water on him, putting out his smoldering clothing. All around debris; bits of brick and gray, dusty mortar. A woman in a black burka approaches in the background, her hands raised to heaven, her mouth open in a wail—Allah!

What I saw that morning was not pretty or romantic, though it was tranquil, as though time had slowed, as though gravity itself increased with each new element of the day falling into place, swirling around the photo on the front page of the *New York Times*.

Let me stop here and say that this is all as I remember it. That day in Erie I saw America with all its attendant myths and legends stripped away. I have taken no liberties, except to organize the experience for you in a way that is free of anything extraneous, so that what you have here is a typical morning in a typical American city, except that it is focused through the lens of a nation at war, a view of the world, which on this one morning, for a few hours, presented itself to me in no uncertain terms from the moment I picked up the newspaper.

There was a sense that the veterans that passed me that day and whom I later saw sitting in the park were aliens to me—mysterious men from an another reality, another America. They were the missing pieces of a puzzle, assembling a picture of the world that I couldn't assemble on my own, not out of a lack of perspective, but because it was a picture I did not care to see.

Having said that, there's something I didn't tell you about that morning, something better left for the end of this story. I left the museum and decided to take a walk down to the park where the Civil War monument stood. Maybe I would catch a glimpse of the veterans I saw before. As I walked I began to think about Erie and what I knew about it. I knew that in the waters off-shore lay the wrecks of more than seventy ships sunk in naval battles and bad weather. As a kid visiting my grandparents, who lived along the lake, I visited monuments dedicated to Commodore Oliver Hazard Perry, the man who lead the American naval fleet in their defeat of a squadron of British ships in the Battle of Lake Erie. But I didn't know much about Lake Erie during the Civil War.

At the park I stood in front of the statue and looked up. Nothing new. Just like the countless other Civil War monuments I'd seen growing up in the Midwest. The plaque in front of the statue, titled "Erie County in the Civil War," said that the Pennsylvania 83rd regiment, made up of citizens from Erie County, suffered the heaviest loss of life of any regiment in the Union army. The USS Michigan, the first steel-hulled warship in the US Navy, was stationed here in Erie harbor during the Civil War. Its primary job was to patrol the waters off of Johnson's Island POW camp, the largest prisoner of war camp in the north, with fifteen-thousand Confederate soldiers detained there over the course of the war. (Later I would find out that over two-hundred prisoners died due to harsh winters, food shortage and disease.) I wrote this down and kept walking.

There was another statue on the far side of the park that I hadn't paid much attention to, and I figured I'd better check it out, just to be thorough. As I walked around the edge of the park I saw some of the men who had passed me earlier sitting together on a pair of facing benches, smoking in the shade of the huge trees.

The statue was of Commodore Perry himself, commemorating the American victory at the Battle of Lake Erie, September 10, 1813. Perry was tall and regal in his braided short coat and tapered trousers. Defiantly, he held aloft a saber, as if shouting, fire! The inscription dedicated the monument to all the Pennsylvanians who built the ships, fought on them and died on them. Beneath this was a quote from Perry. It read: "We have met the enemy and they are ours."

Except someone had crossed out "ours" with a black crayon or perhaps a piece of charcoal and written just below the chiseled word: "Us."

Many thanks are due to Angelo Matera for his guidance and support of this project from the very beginning, as well as for the title of this book. Never ending praise and gratitude to Brett Yasko, the designer of this book. Without you these words wouldn't have seen the light of day. Thanks to Michael Baxter and the Catholic Peace Fellowship for their friendship and Gerard Powers of Notre Dame's Joan B. Kroc Institute for International Peace Studies for opening his classroom to me and giving me valuable knowledge and guidance. Thanks to the Virginia Center for the Creative Arts and the Vira I. Heinz Foundation of Pittsburgh for their support in the early stages of the writing process. Thanks to The Andy Warhol Museum, Linda Benedict-Jones of the Silver Eye Center for Photography and the Erie Museum of Art in Erie, Pennsylvania. Thanks to Luke Gerwe and Rachael Crossland for their invaluable editing skills. Thanks to my first readers: Emily, Bryce, Kelly, Ryan, Christina, Andria and Tom. Thanks to Brandon, Stacey W, Dave C, Mike B, Matt P, Bobby P and Bill K for helping me make it through some tough years. Lastly, thanks to Jess for your unconditional love and support. This book couldn't have been written without you.

David Griffith
01.27.06

New York City
January 14, 2006

"Prime Directive" was originally published in a slightly different form in
Image: A Journal of Religion and the Arts. "A Good War is Hard to Find:
Flannery O'Connor, Abu Ghraib and the Problem of American Innocence"
was originally published in *Godspy* (www.godspy.com).

Design by Brett Yasko (www.brettyasko.com)

Abu Ghraib Prison photographs courtesy of antiwar.com

Published by Soft Skull Press
55 Washington Street, Suite 804
Brooklyn, New York 11201
www.softskull.com

Library of Congress Cataloging-in-Publication Data
Griffith, David A., 1975-
A good war is hard to find : the art of violence in America / by David A. Griffith.
p. cm.
Includes bibliographical references and index.
ISBN 1-933368-12-8 (alk. paper)
1. Violence—United States. 2. Violence in popular culture—United
States. 3. National characteristics, American. I. Title.
HN90.V5G75 2006
303.60973'0904—dc22   2006004051

Printed in Canada